VCLA Virginia Communication and Literacy Assessment

Teacher Certification Exam

By: Sharon Wynne, M.S.
Southern Connecticut State University

"And, while there's no reason yet to panic, I think it's only prudent that we make preparations to panic."

XAMonline, INC.

Boston

To obtain permission(s) to use the material from this work for any purpose including workshops or seminars, please submit a written request to:

XAMonline, Inc.
25 First St. Suite 106
Cambridge, MA 02141
Toll Free 1-800-509-4128
Email: info@xamonline.com
Web www.xamonline.com
Fax: 1-617-583-5552

Library of Congress Cataloging-in-Publication Data

Wynne, Sharon A.
 VCLA Virginia Communication and Literacy Assessment / Sharon A. Wynne. -1st ed.
 ISBN 978-1-60787-1088
 1. Virginia Communication and Literacy Assessment.   2. Study Guides.
 3. VCLA   4. Teachers' Certification & Licensure.   5. Careers

Disclaimer:
The opinions expressed in this publication are the sole works of XAMonline and were created independently from the National Education Association, Educational Testing Service, or any State Department of Education, National Evaluation Systems or other testing affiliates.

Between the time of publication and printing, state specific standards as well as testing formats and website information may change that is not included in part or in whole within this product. Sample test questions are developed by XAMonline and reflect similar content as on real tests; however, they are not former tests. XAMonline assembles content that aligns with state standards but makes no claims nor guarantees teacher candidates a passing score. Numerical scores are determined by testing companies such as NES or ETS and then are compared with individual state standards. A passing score varies from state to state.

Printed in the United States of America   œ-1

VCLA Virginia Communication and Literacy Assessment
ISBN: 978-1-60787-1088

TABLE OF CONTENTS

COMPETENCY 14.0   PREPARE A DEVELOPED COMPOSITION IN A GIVEN TOPIC USING LANGUAGE CONSISTENT WITH A GIVEN AUDIENCE AND PURPOSE.

Great Study and Testing Tips!

What to study in order to prepare for the subject assessments is the focus of this study guide but equally important is *how* you study.

You can increase your chances of truly mastering the information by taking some simple, but effective steps.

Study Tips:

1. **Some foods aid the learning process.** Foods such as milk, nuts, seeds, rice, and oats help your study efforts by releasing natural memory enhancers called CCKs (*cholecystokinin*) composed of *tryptopha*n, *choline*, and *phenylalanine*. All of these chemicals enhance the neurotransmitters associated with memory. Before studying, try a light, protein-rich meal of eggs, turkey, and fish. All of these foods release the memory enhancing chemicals. The better the connections, the more you comprehend.

Likewise, before you take a test, stick to a light snack of energy boosting and relaxing foods. A glass of milk, a piece of fruit, or some peanuts all release various memory-boosting chemicals and help you to relax and focus on the subject at hand.

2. **Learn to take great notes.** A by-product of our modern culture is that we have grown accustomed to getting our information in short doses (i.e. TV news sound bites or USA Today style newspaper articles.)

Consequently, we've subconsciously trained ourselves to assimilate information better in neat little packages. If your notes are scrawled all over the paper, it fragments the flow of the information. Strive for clarity. Newspapers use a standard format to achieve clarity. Your notes can be much clearer through use of proper formatting. A very effective format is called the *"Cornell Method."*

Take a sheet of loose-leaf lined notebook paper and draw a line all the way down the paper about 1-2" from the left-hand edge.

Draw another line across the width of the paper about 1-2" up from the bottom. Repeat this process on the reverse side of the page.

Look at the highly effective result. You have ample room for notes, a left hand margin for special emphasis items or inserting supplementary data from the textbook, a large area at the bottom for a brief summary, and a little rectangular space for just about anything you want.

3. **Get the concept then the details.** Too often we focus on the details and don't gather an understanding of the concept. However, if you simply memorize only dates, places, or names, you may well miss the whole point of the subject.

A key way to understand things is to put them in your own words. If you are working from a textbook, automatically summarize each paragraph in your mind. If you are outlining text, don't simply copy the author's words.

Rephrase them in your own words. You remember your own thoughts and words much better than someone else's, and subconsciously tend to associate the important details to the core concepts.

4. **Ask Why?** Pull apart written material paragraph by paragraph and don't forget the captions under the illustrations.

Example: If the heading is "Stream Erosion", flip it around to read "Why do streams erode?" Then answer the questions.

If you train your mind to think in a series of questions and answers, not only will you learn more, but it also helps to lessen the test anxiety because you are used to answering questions.

5. **Read for reinforcement and future needs.** Even if you only have 10 minutes, put your notes or a book in your hand. Your mind is similar to a computer; you have to input data in order to have it processed. *By reading, you are creating the neural connections for future retrieval.* The more times you read something, the more you reinforce the learning of ideas.

Even if you don't fully understand something on the first pass, *your mind stores much of the material for later recall.*

6. **Relax to learn so go into exile.** Our bodies respond to an inner clock called biorhythms. Burning the midnight oil works well for some people, but not everyone.

If possible, set aside a particular place to study that is free of distractions. Shut off the television, cell phone, and pager and exile your friends and family during your study period.

If you really are bothered by silence, try background music. Light classical music at a low volume has been shown to aid in concentration over other types. Music that evokes pleasant emotions without lyrics is highly suggested. Try just about anything by Mozart. It relaxes you.

7. <u>Use arrows not highlighters</u>. At best, it's difficult to read a page full of yellow, pink, blue, and green streaks. Try staring at a neon sign for a while and you'll soon see that the horde of colors obscure the message.

A quick note, a brief dash of color, an underline, and an arrow pointing to a particular passage is much clearer than a horde of highlighted words.

8. <u>Budget your study time</u>. Although you shouldn't ignore any of the material, *allocate your available study time in the same ratio that topics may appear on the test.*

Testing Tips:

1. <u>**Get smart, play dumb**</u>. **Don't read anything into the question.** Don't make an assumption that the test writer is looking for something else than what is asked. Stick to the question as written and don't read extra things into it.

2. <u>**Read the question and all the choices**</u> *twice* <u>**before answering the**</u> <u>**question**</u>. You may miss something by not carefully reading, and then re-reading both the question and the answers.

If you really don't have a clue as to the right answer, leave it blank on the first time through. Go on to the other questions, as they may provide a clue as to how to answer the skipped questions.

If later on, you still can't answer the skipped ones . . . *Guess.* The only penalty for guessing is that you *might* get it wrong. Only one thing is certain; if you don't put anything down, you will get it wrong!

3. <u>**Turn the question into a statement**</u>. Look at the way the questions are worded. The syntax of the question usually provides a clue. Does it seem more familiar as a statement rather than as a question? Does it sound strange?

By turning a question into a statement, you may be able to spot if an answer sounds right, and it may also trigger memories of material you have read.

4. <u>**Look for hidden clues**</u>. It's actually very difficult to compose multiple-foil (choice) questions without giving away part of the answer in the options presented.

In most multiple-choice questions you can often readily eliminate one or two of the potential answers. This leaves you with only two real possibilities and automatically your odds go to Fifty-Fifty for very little work.

5. <u>**Trust your instincts**</u>. For every fact that you have read, you subconsciously retain something of that knowledge. On questions that you aren't really certain about, go with your basic instincts. **Your first impression on how to answer a question is usually correct.**

6. <u>**Mark your answers directly on the test booklet**</u>. Don't bother trying to fill in the optical scan sheet on the first pass through the test.

Just be very careful not to miss-mark your answers when you eventually transcribe them to the scan sheet.

7. <u>**Watch the clock**</u>! You have a set amount of time to answer the questions. Don't get bogged down trying to answer a single question at the expense of 10 questions you can more readily answer.

THIS PAGE BLANK

DOMAIN I.   **READING COMPREHENSION AND ANALYSIS**

COMPETENCY 1.0   **UNDERSTAND THE MEANING OF WORDS AND PHRASES.**

Skill 1.1   **Use context clues to determine the meaning of a word with multiple meanings.**

Context clues help readers determine the meanings of unfamiliar words. The context of a word is the sentence or sentences that surround the word.

Read the following sentences, and attempt to determine the meanings of the words in bold print.

> The **luminosity** of the room was so incredible that there was no need for lights.

If there were no need for lights, then one must assume that the word luminosity has something to do with giving off light. The definition of luminosity is *the emission of light*.

> Jamie could not understand Joe's feelings. His mood swings made understanding him somewhat of an **enigma.**

The fact that he could not be understood made him somewhat of a puzzle. The definition of enigma is *a mystery or puzzle*.

Familiarity with word **roots** (the basic elements of words) and with **prefixes** can help one determine the meanings of unknown words. Following is a partial list of roots and prefixes. It might be useful to review these.

Root	Meaning	Example
aqua	water	aqualung
astro	stars	astrology
bio	life	biology
carn	meat	carnivorous
circum	around	circumnavigate
geo	earth	geology
herb	plant	herbivorous
mal	bad	malicious
neo	new	neonatal
tele	distant	telescope
un-	not	unnamed
re-	again	reenter
il-	not	illegible
pre-	before	preset
mis-	incorrectly	misstate
in-	not	informal
anti-	against	antiwar
de-	opposite	derail
post-	after	postwar
ir-	not	irresponsible

Word Forms

Sometimes a very familiar word can appear as a different part of speech. For example, you may have heard that *fraud* involves a criminal misrepresentation, so when it appears as the adjective form *fraudulent*, (e.g., "He was suspected of *fraudulent* activities.") you can make an educated guess. You probably know that something out-of-date is *obsolete;* therefore, when you read about "built-in *obsolescence,*" you can detect the meaning of the unfamiliar word.

Practice Questions: Read the following sentences and attempt to determine the meanings of the underlined words.

1.   Farmer John got a two-horse plow and went to work. Straight <u>furrows</u> stretched out behind him.

   The word <u>furrows</u> means

   (A) long cuts made by a plow
   (B) vast, open fields
   (C) rows of corn
   (D) pairs of hitched horses

2.   The survivors struggled ahead, <u>shambling</u> through the terrible cold, doing their best not to fall.

   The word <u>shambling</u> means

   (A) frozen in place
   (B) running
   (C) shivering uncontrollably
   (D) walking awkwardly

Answers:

1. (A) is the correct answer. The word *straight* and the expression *stretched out behind him* are your clues.

2. (D) is the correct answer. The words *ahead* and *through* are your clues.

Skill 1.2   Use the context of a paragraph or passage to determine the meaning of words or phrases.

Adjacent sentence clues

The context for a word goes beyond the sentence in which it appears. At times, the writer uses adjacent (adjoining) sentences to present an explanation or definition.

   The two dollars for the car repair would have to come out of the <u>contingency</u> fund. Fortunately, Angela's father had taught her to keep some money set aside for just such emergencies.

Analysis: The second sentence offers a clue to the definition of *contingency* as used in this sentence—*emergencies*. Therefore, a fund for contingencies would be money tucked away for unforeseen and/or urgent events.

Entire passage clues

On occasion, you must look at an entire paragraph or passage to figure out the definition of a word or term. In the following paragraph, notice how the word *nostalgia* undergoes a form of extended definition throughout the selection rather than in just one sentence.

> The word <u>nostalgia</u> links Greek words for "away from home" and "pain." If you are feeling <u>nostalgic</u>, then you are probably in some physical distress or discomfort, suffering from a feeling of alienation and separation from loved ones or loved places. <u>Nostalgia</u> is that awful feeling you remember the first time you went away to camp or spent the weekend with a friend's family—homesickness, or some condition even more painful than that. However, in common use, <u>nostalgia</u> has come to have associations that are more sentimental. A few years back, for example, a <u>nostalgia</u> craze had to do with the 1950s. We resurrected poodle skirts and saddle shoes, built new restaurants to look like old ones, and tried to make chicken à la king just as mother probably never made it. In TV situation comedies, we recreated a pleasant world that probably never existed and relished our <u>nostalgia</u>, longing for a homey, comfortable lost time.

Skill 1.3   Identify synonyms or antonyms for words in a passage.

The context for a word is the written passage that surrounds it. Sometimes the writer offers synonyms—words that have nearly the same meaning. Context clues can appear within the sentence itself, within the preceding and/or following sentence(s), or in the passage as a whole.

Sentence clues

Often, a writer will actually **define** a difficult or particularly important word for you the first time it appears in a passage. Phrases such as *that is, such as, which is,* or *is called* might announce the writer's intention to give just the definition you need. Occasionally, a writer will simply use a synonym (a word that means the same thing) or a near-synonym joined by the word *or.* Look at the following examples:

> The <u>credibility</u>, that is to say the believability, of the witness was called into question by evidence of previous perjury.

> Nothing would <u>assuage</u> or lessen the child's grief.

Punctuation at the sentence level is often a clue to the meaning of a word. Commas, parentheses, quotation marks, and dashes tell the reader that the writer is offering a definition.

> *A tendency toward <u>hyperbole</u>, extravagant exaggeration, is a common flaw among persuasive writers.*

> *Political <u>apathy</u>—lack of interest—can lead to the death of the state.*

A writer might simply give an **explanation** in other words that you can understand in the same sentence.

> *The <u>xenophobic</u> townspeople were suspicious of every foreigner.*

Writers also explain a word in terms of its **opposite** at the sentence level.

> *His <u>incarceration</u> was ended, and he was elated to be out of jail.*

COMPETENCY 2.0   UNDERSTAND THE MAIN IDEA AND SUPPORTING DETAILS IN WRITTEN MATERIAL.

Skill 2.1   Identify the main idea of a paragraph or passage.

Main Idea

The main idea of a passage or paragraph is the basic message, idea, point concept, or meaning that the author wants to convey to you, the reader. Understanding the main idea of a passage or paragraph is the key to understanding the more subtle components of the author's message. The main idea is what is being said about a topic or subject. Once you have identified the basic message, you will have an easier time answering other questions that test critical skills.

Main ideas are either *stated* or *implied*. A *stated main idea* is explicit; it is directly expressed in a sentence or two in the paragraph or passage. An *implied main idea* is suggested by the overall reading selection. In the first case, you need not pull information from various points in the paragraph or passage in order to form the main idea because the author already states it. If a main idea is implied, however, you must formulate, in your own words, a main idea statement by condensing the overall message contained in the material itself.

Practice Question: Read the following passage and select an answer.

> *Sometimes too much of a good thing can become a very bad thing indeed. In an earnest attempt to consume a healthy diet, dietary supplement enthusiasts have been known to overdose. Vitamin C, for example, long thought to help people ward off cold viruses, is currently being studied for its possible role in warding off cancer and other disease that causes tissue degeneration. Unfortunately, an overdose of vitamin C—more than 10 mg—on a daily basis can cause nausea and diarrhea. Calcium supplements, commonly taken by women, are helpful in warding off osteoporosis. More than just a few grams a day, however, can lead to stomach upset and even kidney and bladder stones. Niacin, proven useful in reducing cholesterol levels, can be dangerous in large doses to those who suffer from heart problems, asthma, or ulcers.*

The main idea expressed in this paragraph is

A.   Supplements taken in excess can be a bad thing indeed.
B.   Dietary supplement enthusiasts have been known to overdose.
C.   Vitamins can cause nausea, diarrhea, and kidney or bladder stones.
D.   People who take supplements are preoccupied with their health.

Answer: Answer A is a paraphrase of the first sentence and provides a general framework for the rest of the paragraph—excess supplement intake is bad. The rest of the paragraph discusses the consequences of taking too many vitamins. Options B and C refer to major details and Option D introduces the idea of preoccupation, which is not included in this paragraph.

Skill 2.2   Establish the sequence of events or steps presented in a passage.

Sequence of Events
The ability to organize events or steps provided in a passage (especially when presented in random order) serves a useful purpose, and it encourages the development of logical thinking and the processes of analysis and evaluation.

One way to identify sequence is to note transition words, such as "first" or "then." Another clue is to use enumeration to identify the proper order.

Working through and discussing examples, such as the one below, with your students helps students to gain valuable practice in sequencing events.

Practice Question: Identify the proper order of events or steps.

1. Matt had tied a knot in his shoelace.
2. Matt put on his green socks because they were clean and complemented the brown slacks he was wearing.
3. Matt took a bath and trimmed his toenails.
4. Matt put on his brown slacks.

Answer: The proper order of events is 3, 4, 2, and 1.

Skill 2.3   Recognize information, ideas, and details that support the main idea of a paragraph or passage.

Supporting details
Supporting details are examples, facts, ideas, illustrations, cases, and anecdotes used by a writer to explain, expand on, and develop the more general main idea. A writer's choice of supporting materials is determined by the nature of the topic being covered. Supporting details are specifics that relate directly to the main idea.

Writers select and shape material according to their purposes. An advertisement writer seeking to persuade the reader to buy a particular running shoe, for instance, will emphasize only the positive characteristics of the shoe for advertisement copy. A columnist for a running magazine, on the other hand, might list the good and bad points about the same shoe in an article recommending appropriate shoes for different kinds of runners. Both major details (those that directly support the main idea) and minor details (those that provide interesting, but not always essential, information) help create a well-written and fluid passage.

In the following paragraph, the sentences in **bold print** provide a skeleton of a paragraph on the benefits of recycling. The sentences in bold are generalizations, which by themselves do not explain the need to recycle. The sentences in *italics* add details to SHOW the general points in bold. Notice how the supporting details help you understand the necessity for recycling.

> **While one day recycling may become mandatory in all states, right now it is voluntary in many communities.** *Those of us who participate in recycling are amazed by how much material is recycled.* **For many communities, the blue-box recycling program has had an immediate effect.** *By just recycling glass, aluminum cans, and plastic bottles, we have reduced the volume of disposable trash by one third, thus extending the useful life of local landfills by over a decade. Imagine the difference if those dramatic results were achieved nationwide.* **The amount of reusable items we thoughtlessly dispose of is staggering.** *For example, Americans dispose of enough steel everyday to supply Detroit car manufacturers for three months. Additionally, we dispose of enough aluminum annually to rebuild the nation's air fleet. These statistics, available from the Environmental Protection Agency (EPA), should encourage all of us to watch what we throw away.* **Clearly, recycling in our homes and in our communities directly improves the environment.**

Notice how the author's supporting examples enhance the message of the paragraph and relate to the author's thesis noted above. If you only read the boldfaced sentences, you have a glimpse at the topic. This paragraph of illustration, however, is developed through numerous details creating specific images: *reduced the volume of disposable trash by one-third, extended the useful life of local landfills by over a decade, enough steel everyday to supply Detroit car manufacturers for three months, enough aluminum to rebuild the nation's air fleet.* If the writer had merely written a few general sentences, as those shown in bold print, you would not fully understand the vast amount of trash involved in recycling or the positive results of current recycling efforts.

Skill 2.4   **Recognize a writer's expressed or implied purpose for writing (e.g., to persuade, to describe).**

Writer's purpose

An essay is an extended discussion of a writer's point of view about a particular topic. This point of view may be supported by using such writing modes as examples, argument and persuasion, analysis, or comparison/contrast. In any case, a good essay is clear, coherent, well organized, and fully developed.

When an author sets out to write a passage, he/she usually has a purpose for doing so. That purpose may be simply to give information that might be interesting or useful to some reader or other. It may be to persuade the reader to a point of view or to move the reader to act in a particular way. It may be to tell a story, or it may be to describe something in such a way that an experience becomes available to the reader through one of the five senses. Following are the primary devices for expressing a particular purpose in a piece of writing:

- **Basic expository writing** simply gives information not previously known about a topic or is used to explain or define one. Facts, examples, statistics, cause and effect, direct tone, objective rather than subjective delivery, and non-emotional information are presented in a formal manner.

- **Descriptive writing** centers on a person, place, or object, using concrete and sensory words to create a mood or impression and arranging details in a chronological or spatial sequence.

- **Narrative writing** is developed using an incident or anecdote or related series of events. Chronology, the five W's, topic sentence, and conclusion are essential ingredients.

- **Persuasive writing** implies the writer's ability to select vocabulary and arrange facts and opinions in such a way as to direct the actions of the listener/reader. Persuasive writing may incorporate exposition and narration as they illustrate the main idea.

- **Journalistic writing** is theoretically free of author bias. It is essential that it be factual and objective when relaying information about an event, person, or thing. Provide students with an opportunity to examine newspapers and create their own. Many newspapers have educational programs that are offered free to schools.

COMPETENCY 3.0   **ANALYZE THE RELATIONSHIP AMONG IDEAS IN WRITTEN MATERIAL.**

Skill 3.1   Recognize cause-and-effect relationships in a passage.

A cause is the necessary source of a particular outcome. If a writer were addressing the questions, "How will the new tax laws affect small businesses?" or "Why has there been such political unrest in Somalia?" he or she would use cause and effect as an organizational pattern to structure his or her response. In the first case, the writer would emphasize effects of the tax legislation as they apply to owners of small businesses. In the second, he/she would focus on causes for the current political situation in Somalia.

Some word clues that identify a cause-effect passage are *accordingly, as a result, therefore, because, consequently, hence, in short, thus, then, due to* and *so on.*

Sample passage:

> *Simply put, inflation is an increase in price levels. It happens when a government prints more currency than is already in circulation, and there is, consequently, additional money available for the same amount of goods or services. There might be multiple reasons for a government to crank up the printing presses. A war, for instance, could cause an immediate need for steel. A national disaster might create a sudden need for social services. To get the money it needs, a government can raise taxes, borrow, or print more currency. However, raising taxes and borrowing are not always plausible options.*

Analysis: The paragraph starts with a definition and proceeds to examine a causal chain. The words *consequently, reasons,* and *cause* provide the clues.

Explicit Cause and Effect

General Hooker failed to anticipate General Lee's bold flanking maneuver. As a result, Hooker's army was nearly routed by a smaller force.

Mindy forgot to bring the lunch her father had packed for her. Consequently, she had to borrow money from her friends at school during lunch period.

Implicit Cause and Effect

The engine in Lisa's airplane began to sputter. She quickly looked below for a field in which to land.

Luther ate the creamed shrimp that had been sitting in the sun for hours. Later that night, he was so sick he had to be rushed to the hospital.

Whenever there are two ideas in opposition, there is the ghost of an "either/or" conceptual basis lurking invisibly in the background of the "pro/con" setting.

For example, one person may argue that automobiles are a safer mode of transportation than are motorcycles and support that contention with statistics showing that fatalities are more frequent per accident in motorcycle crashes than in car crashes.

Skill 3.2 Analyze relationships between ideas in opposition (e.g., pro and con) or in agreement (e.g., reasons to support a claim).

Opposition to argument

The opposition to this argument may counter that while fatalities are more frequent per accident in motorcycle accidents, it is erroneous to over generalize from that statistic that motorcycles are "therefore more dangerous."

Thus, each participant in the argument has assumed a position of "either/or," that is to say, the automobile is "either" safer than the motorcycle, "or" it is not (or the motorcycle is "either" safer than the automobile, "or" it is not). With the argument thus formulated, a conclusion acceptable to both sides is not likely to happen. Here is a short essay showing how to avoid this deadlock.

Which is safer—the car or the motorcycle?

Most experienced drivers would agree that while it is more exhilarating to ride a motorcycle than to drive an automobile, it is illogical to therefore conclude that this exhilaration leads to careless driving and, therefore, more accidents, deaths, and injuries to motorcycle riders than car drivers. The critical concept to be understood here is not exhilaration, which is a given, but how the exhilaration comes about and is a cause of serious injury and death of motorcycle riders.

There is safe and unsafe thrill seeking. "Exhilaration" is defined as the "state of being stimulated, refreshed, or elated." An example of safe exhilaration is the excitement of sledding downhill, which results in the sled rider feeling stimulated, refreshed, and/or elated.

Unsafe exhilaration, which is usually the consequence of reckless thrill seeking, is therefore a state of being over-stimulated, frightened, and depressed by terror.

Which then causes exhilaration that is more dangerous, the car or the motorcycle? The answer is that the two forms of exhilaration are the consequences not of the motorcycle or the automobile, per se, but of the operation of the respective vehicles. Without an operator, both vehicles are metal entities, sitting in space, neither threatening nor harmful to anyone.

Therefore, neither the motorcycle nor the car is more or less dangerous than the other is; it is the attitude of their operators that creates the danger, death, and dismemberment resultant from accidents.

Notice how the writer has avoided the logical trap of the "either/or" construction built into the "pro/con" argument by defining the key term "exhilaration" to clarify the issue (and to shift the focus to the operator). He also resolves the either/or dilemma by arguing that it is the operators of the vehicles, not the vehicles themselves, that are responsible for negative consequences.

Skill 3.3   Draw conclusions from information stated or implied in a passage.

An **inference** is sometimes called an *educated guess* because it requires that you go beyond the strictly obvious to create additional meaning by taking the text one logical step further. Inferences and conclusions are based on the content of the passage—that is, on what the passage says or how the writer says it—and are derived by reasoning. Inference is an essential and automatic component of most reading. Examples include making educated guesses about the meaning of unknown words, the author's main idea, or the presence of bias in his or her writing. Such is the essence of inference—you use your own ability to reason in order to figure out what the writer implies. As a reader, then, you must often logically extend meaning that is only implied.

Consider the following example. Assume you are an employer, and you are reading over the letters of reference submitted by a prospective employee for the position of clerk/typist in your real estate office. The position requires the applicant to be neat, careful, trustworthy, and punctual. You come across this letter of reference submitted by an applicant.

> *To Whom It May Concern:*
>
> *Todd Finley has asked me to write a letter of reference for him. I am well qualified to do so because he worked for me for three months last year. His duties included answering the phone, greeting the public, and producing some simple memos and notices on the computer. Although Todd initially had few computer skills and little knowledge of telephone etiquette, he did acquire some during his stay with us. Todd's manner of speaking, both on the telephone and with the clients who came to my establishment, could be described as casual. He was particularly effective when communicating with peers. Please contact me by telephone if you wish to have further information about my experience with Todd.*

Here the writer implies, rather than openly states, the main idea. This letter calls attention to itself because there is a problem with its tone. A truly positive letter would say something such as, "I have the distinct honor of recommending Todd Finley." Here, however, the letter simply verifies that Todd worked in the office. Second, the praise is obviously lukewarm. For example, the writer says that Todd "was particularly effective when communicating with peers." An educated guess translates that statement into a nice way of saying Todd was not serious about his communication with clients.

In order to draw **inferences** and make **conclusions**, a reader must use prior knowledge and apply it to the current situation. A conclusion or inference is never stated. You must rely on your common sense.

Practice Questions: Read the following passages and select an answer.

1. Tim Sullivan had just turned fifteen. As a birthday present, his parents had given him a guitar and a certificate for ten guitar lessons. He had always shown a love of music and a desire to learn an instrument. Tim began his lessons, and before long, he was making up his own songs. At the music studio, Tim met Josh, who played the piano, and Roger, whose instrument was the saxophone. They all shared the same dream, to start a band, and each was praised by his teacher as having real talent.

   From this passage, one can infer that

   A. Tim, Roger, and Josh are going to start their own band.
   B. Tim is going to give up his guitar lessons.
   C. Tim, Josh, and Roger will no longer be friends.
   D. Josh and Roger are going to start their own band.

2. The Smith family waited patiently around carousel number 7 for their luggage to arrive. They were exhausted after their five-hour trip and were anxious to get to their hotel. After about an hour, they realized that they no longer recognized any of the other passengers' faces. Mrs. Smith asked the person who appeared to be in charge if they were at the right carousel. The man replied, "Yes, this is it, but we finished unloading that baggage almost half an hour ago."

   From the man's response, we can infer that

   A. The Smiths were ready to go to their hotel.
   B. The Smiths' luggage was lost.
   C. The man had their luggage.
   D. They were at the wrong carousel.

Answers:

1. A is the correct choice. Given the facts that Tim wanted to be a musician and start his own band, after meeting others who shared the same dreams, we can infer that they joined in an attempt to make their dreams become a reality.

2. Since the Smiths were still waiting for their luggage, we know that they were not yet ready to go to their hotel. From the man's response, we know that they were not at the wrong carousel and that he did not have their luggage. Therefore, though not directly stated, it appears that their luggage was lost. Choice B is the correct answer.

COMPETENCY 4.0   **USE CRITICAL-REASONING SKILLS TO EVALUATE WRITTEN MATERIAL.**

Skill 4.1   **Interpret a passage to determine the writer's opinion, point of view, or position on an issue.**

The **tone** of a written passage is the author's attitude toward the subject matter. The tone (mood, feeling) is revealed through the qualities of the writing itself and is a direct product of such stylistic elements as language and sentence structure. The tone of the written passage is much like a speaker's voice; instead of being spoken, however, it is the product of words on a page.

Often, writers have an emotional stake in the subject, and their purpose, either explicitly or implicitly, is to convey those feelings to the reader. In such cases, the writing is generally subjective; that is, it stems from opinions, judgments, values, ideas, and feelings. Both sentence structure (syntax) and word choice (diction) are instrumental tools in creating tone.

Tone may be thought of generally as positive, negative, or neutral. Below is a statement about snakes that demonstrates this.

> *Many species of snakes live in Florida. Some of those species, both poisonous and non-poisonous, have habitats that coincide with those of human residents of the state.*

The voice of the writer in this statement is neutral. The sentences are declarative (not exclamations or fragments or questions). The adjectives are few and nondescript—*many, some, poisonous* (balanced with *non-poisonous).* Nothing much in this brief paragraph would alert the reader to the feelings of the writer about snakes. The paragraph has a neutral, objective, detached, impartial tone.

Then again, if the writer's attitude towards snakes involves admiration, or even affection, the tone would generally be positive.

> *Florida's snakes are a tenacious bunch. When they find their habitats invaded by humans, they cling to their home territories as long as they can, as if vainly attempting to fight off the onslaught of the human hordes.*

An additional message emerges in this paragraph—the writer quite clearly favors snakes over people. The writer uses adjectives such as *tenacious* to describe his/her feelings about snakes. The writer also humanizes the reptiles, making them brave, beleaguered creatures. Obviously, the writer is more sympathetic to snakes than to people in this paragraph.

If the writer's attitude toward snakes involves active dislike and fear, then the tone would also reflect that attitude by being negative.

> *Countless species of snakes, some more dangerous than others, still lurk on the urban fringes of Florida's towns and cities. They will often invade domestic spaces, terrorizing people and their pets.*

Here, obviously, the snakes are the villains. They *lurk,* they *invade,* and they *terrorize.* The tone of this paragraph might be said to be distressed about snakes.

In the same manner, a writer can use language to portray characters as good or bad. A writer uses positive and negative adjectives, as seen above, to convey the manner of a character.

Bias is defined as an opinion, feeling, or influence that strongly favors one side in an argument. A statement or passage is biased if an author attempts to convince a reader of something.

Is there evidence of bias in the following statement?

> *Using a calculator cannot help a student understand the process of graphing, so its use is a waste of time.*

Since the author makes it perfectly clear that he does not favor the use of the calculator in graphing problems, the answer is yes, there is evidence of bias. He has included his opinion in this statement.

Practice Question: Read the following paragraph and select an answer.

There are teachers who feel that computer programs are quite useful in helping students grasp certain math concepts. There are also those who disagree with this feeling. It is up to each individual math teacher to decide if computer programs benefit her particular group of students.

Is there evidence of bias in this paragraph?

(A) yes
(B) no

Answer: B is the correct answer. The author seems to state both sides of the argument without favoring a particular side.

"The sky is blue," and "The sky looks like rain"; one is a fact, and the other, an opinion. This is because one is **readily provable by objective empirical data**, while the other is a **subjective evaluation based upon personal bias**. This means that facts are things that can be proved by the usual means of study and experimentation. We can look and see the color of the sky. Since the shade we are observing is expressed as the color blue and is an accepted norm, the observation that *the sky is blue* is therefore a fact. (Of course, this depends on other external factors, such as time and weather conditions.)

This brings us to our next idea—that it looks like rain. This is a subjective observation, in that an individual's perception will differ from another's. What looks like rain to one person will not necessarily look like that to another person. The question thus remains as to how to differentiate fact from opinion. The best and only way is to ask oneself if what is being stated can be proved from other sources, by other methods, or by the simple process of **reasoning**.

Skill 4.2   Analyze the stated or implied assumptions on which the validity of an argument depends.

The terms **valid** and **invalid** have special meaning. If an argument is valid, it is reasonable. It is objective (not biased) and can be supported by evidence. If an argument is invalid, it is not reasonable. It is not objective. In other words, one can find evidence of bias.

Practice Questions: Read the following passage and select an answer.

1.   Most dentists agree that Bright Smile Toothpaste is the best for fighting cavities. It tastes good and leaves your mouth minty fresh.

    Is this a valid or invalid argument?

    (A) valid
    (B) invalid

2.   It is difficult to decide who will make the best presidential candidate, Senator Johnson or Senator Keeley. They have both been involved in scandals and have both gone through messy divorces while in office.

    Is this argument valid or invalid?

    (A) valid
    (B) invalid

Answers:

1. It is invalid (B). It mentions that "most" dentists agree. What about those who do not agree? The author is clearly exhibiting bias in leaving out those who disagree.

2. A is the correct choice. The author appears to be listing facts. He does not seem to favor one candidate over the other.

It is important to assess continually whether or not a sentence contributes to the overall task of supporting the main idea. When a sentence is deemed irrelevant, it is best either to omit it from the passage or to make it relevant by one of the following strategies:

1. Adding detail—Sometimes a sentence can seem out of place if it does not contain enough information to link it to the topic. Adding specific information can show how the sentence is related to the main idea.

2. Adding an example—This is especially important in passages in which information is being argued, compared, or contrasted. Examples can support the main idea and give the document overall credibility.

3. Using diction effectively—It is important to understand connotation, avoid ambiguity, and avoid too much repetition when selecting words.

4. Adding transitions—Transitions are extremely helpful for making sentences relevant because they are specifically designed to connect one idea to another. They can also reduce a paragraph's choppiness.

Skill 4.3   Analyze the logical structure of an argument and identify instances of faulty reasoning.

An argument by analogy states that if two things have one thing in common, they probably have other things in common. For example, peaches and plums are both fruits that have chemicals good for people to eat. Both peaches and plums are circular in shape; thus, it could be argued by analogy that *because* something is circular in shape, it is fruit and something good for people to eat. However, this analogical deduction is not logical (e.g., a baseball is circular in shape but hardly good to eat).

An analogy is a comparison of the likenesses of two things. The danger of arguing by analogy rests in a failure to perceive correctly the limitations of the likenesses between the two things compared. Because something is like something else does not make it the same as the compared object or, for that matter, put it in the same class as the original object.

For example, a false argument based on analogical thinking could go like this: "Blake and Blunder are both democrats. Both are married. Both have three children, a dog, and a kitten at home. Therefore, it is likely they will both vote the same way about the school mileage proposal because of their similarities."

This is a false argument by analogy. While the likenesses cited are somewhat striking, these are only likenesses coincidental in nature and not compelling causative roots predictive of behaviors.

However, perceiving the analogical relationship between two things or phenomena is often also the starting point for scientific investigations of reality, and such perceptions are the subjects of a host of scientific theories (e.g., the work of Charles Darwin) and investigations (e.g., wave/particle theories in quantum physics). Such analogical relations require austere scrutiny and analysis, and without such, are essentially meaningless or the stuff of poetic comparisons *("To see the world in a grain of sand"*—William Blake).

Thinking in analogies is the way we all began as children to perceive the world and sort it into categories of *good* and *bad* (e.g., "water is a liquid that is good for me; hot oil is a liquid that is bad for me"). Mature writers and thinkers discriminate carefully between all elements of an argument by analogy.

Skill 4.4   Distinguish between fact and opinion in written material.

Facts are verifiable statements. Opinions are statements, such as beliefs, values, judgments, or feelings, which must be supported in order to be accepted, Facts are objective statements used to support subjective opinions. For example, "Jane is a bad girl" is an opinion. However, "Jane hit her sister with a baseball bat" is a *fact* upon which the opinion is based. Judgments are opinions—decisions or declarations based on observation or reasoning—that express approval or disapproval. Facts report what has happened or exists and come from observation, measurement, or calculation. Facts can be tested and verified, whereas opinions and judgments cannot. They can only be supported with facts.

Most statements cannot be so clearly distinguished. "I believe that Jane is a bad girl" is a fact. The speaker knows what he/she believes. However, it obviously includes a judgment that could be disputed by another person who might believe otherwise. Judgments are not usually so firm. They are, rather, plausible opinions that provoke thought or lead to factual development.

Mickey Mantle replaced Joe DiMaggio, a Yankees' centerfielder, in 1952.

This is a fact. If necessary, evidence can be produced to support this.

First year players are more ambitious than seasoned players are.

This is an opinion. There is no proof to support that everyone feels this way.

Practice Questions: Decide if the statement is fact or opinion.

1. The Inca were a group of Indians who ruled an empire in South America.

   (A) fact
   (B) opinion

2. The Inca were clever.

   (A) fact
   (B) opinion

3. The Inca built very complex systems of bridges.

   (A) fact
   (B) opinion

Answers:

1. A is the correct answer. Research can prove this true.
2. B is the correct answer. It is doubtful that all people who have studied the Inca agree with this statement. Therefore, no proof is available.
3. A is the correct answer. As with question number one, research can prove this true.

COMPETENCY 5.0 **APPLY SKILLS FOR SUMMARIZING, OUTLINING, AND VISUALLY REPRESENTING WRITTEN MATERIALS AND FOR INTERPRETING INFORMATION PRESENTED IN GRAPHIC FORM.**

Skill 5.1 **Identify an accurate summary, outline, or graphic representation of information presented in written material.**

One way to determine the understanding of your students is to have them summarize a passage. To do so, they must be able to determine the main ideas and supporting details and then identify the underlying structure.

Summary skills can be developed through practice and repetition. Here's an example:

Sample Passage

Chili peppers may turn out to be the wonder drug of the decade. The fiery fruit comes in many sizes, shapes, and colors, all of which grow on plants that are genetic descendants of the tepin plant, originally native to the Americas. Connoisseurs of the regional cuisines of the Southwest and Louisiana are already well aware that food flavored with chilies can cause a good sweat, but medical researchers are learning more every day about the medical power of capsaicin, the ingredient in the peppers that produces the heat.

Capsaicin as a pain medication has been a part of fold medicine for centuries. It is, in fact, the active ingredient in several currently available over-the-counter liniments for sore muscles. Recent research has been examining the value of the compound for the treatment of other painful conditions. Capsaicin shows some promise in the treatment of phantom limb syndrome, as well as shingles and some types of headaches. Additional research focuses upon the use of capsaicin to relieve pain in post-surgical patients. Scientists speculate that application of the compound to the skin causes the body to release endorphins—natural pain relievers manufactured by the body itself. An alternative theory holds that capsaicin somehow interferes with the transmission of signals along the nerve fibers, thus reducing the sensation of pain.

In addition to its well-documented history as a painkiller, capsaicin has recently received attention as a phytochemical, one of the naturally occurring compounds from foods that show cancer-fighting qualities. Like the phytochemical sulfoaphane found in broccoli, capsaicin might turn out to be an agent capable of short-circuiting the actions of carcinogens at the cell level before they can cause cancer.

Summary: Chili peppers contain a chemical called capsaicin, which has proved useful for treating a variety of ailments. Recent research reveals that capsaicin is a phytochemical, a natural compound that may help fight cancer.

Outlines

In outline information, it is crucial to identify the headings and subheadings for the topic. When researching information, it is easier to cut and paste information under the indicated headings in creating a visual flow of information for the report. In the actual drafting of the report, the writer is able to lift direct quotations and citations from the posted information to incorporate in the writing.

Using the same passage above, this informal outline identifies the main idea and supporting details.

Outline: -Chili peppers could be the wonder drug of the decade.
-Chili peppers contain capsaicin.
-Capsaicin can be used as a pain medication.
-Capsaicin is a phytochemical.
-Phytochemicals show cancer-fighting qualities.
-Capsaicin might be able to short-circuit the effects of carcinogens.

Mapping

Mapping is a strategy that can be used to reach all learning styles, and therefore is an important one to teach. It is exactly what its name implies—a map of the reading. A map helps the reader maneuver through the information in a meaningful manner. Maps can use words with key ideas connected to smaller chunks of information. Teachers can also encourage pictures instead of words to help the visual learner. Adding color to a map can help certain ideas stand out more. This can be particularly helpful for students to begin to understand the process of prioritization in skills. Combining words and pictures is probably the most commonly used type of map. Lines are drawn between connecting concepts to show relationships, and because the reader is creating it himself or herself, it is meaningful. Maps are individual creations and revolve around the reader's learning and prior knowledge.

Skill 5.2   Interpret information presented in charts, graphs, or tables.

Visuals are an effective and dynamic way to add meaning to a text. They can clarify meaning, emphasize important data, summarize points, and add visual appeal. More often, they supplement the written text rather than stand independent. Learning how to interpret the data in various graphics is an important skill for students.

Some possibilities for the analysis of data whether presented in tables, charts, graphs, maps, or other illustrations are as follow:

- Qualitative descriptions: Would drawing conclusions about the quality of a particular treatment or course of action be revealed by the illustration?
- Quantitative descriptions: How much do the results of one particular treatment or course of action differ from another one, and is that variation significant?
- Classification: Is worthwhile information derived from breaking the information down into classifications?
- Estimations: Is it possible to estimate future performance on the basis of the information in the illustration?
- Comparisons: Is it useful to make comparisons based on the data?
- Relationships. Are relationships between components revealed by the scrutiny of the data?
- Cause-and-effect relationships: Is it suggested by the data that there were cause-and-effect relationships that were not previously apparent?
- Mapping and modeling: If the data were mapped and a model drawn up, would the point of the document be demonstrated or refuted?

Questions to ask regarding an illustration: Why is it in this document? What was the writer's purpose in putting it in the document and why at this particular place? Does it make a point clearer? What implications are inherent in a table that shows birth statistics in all states or even in some selected states? What does that have to do with the point and purpose of this piece of writing? Is there adequate preparation in the text for the inclusion of the illustration? Does the illustration underscore or clarify any of the points made in the text? Is there a clear connection between the illustration and the subject matter of the text?

Skill 5.3 **Select graphic forms (e.g., bar graphs, line graphs, pie charts, tables, timelines, graphic organizers) to present information contained in written material.**

Choosing the appropriate graphic form depends on the type of information and data. For example, a pie chart that shows parts of a whole would not be useful for showing trends over time. A line chart rather than a bar chart is more effective when showing the interaction of two variables.

- **Tables**
  Tables depict exact numbers and other data in rows and columns. Those that simply store descriptive information in a form available for general use are called repository tables. They usually contain primary data, which simply summarize raw data. They are not intended to analyze the data, so any analysis is left to the reader or user of the table. A good example of a repository table would be a report of birth statistics by the federal Health and Human Services Department. An analytical table, on the other hand, is constructed from some sort of analysis of primary or secondary data, possibly from a repository table or from the raw data itself. An example of an analytical table would be one that compares birth statistics in 1980 to birth statistics in 2005 for the country at large. It might also break the data down into comparisons by state.

- **Graphs**
  Graphs depict trends, movements, distributions, and cycles more readily than tables. While graphs can present statistics in a more interesting and comprehensible form than tables, they are less accurate. For this reason, the two will often be shown together.

- **Maps**
  While the most obvious use for maps is to locate places geographically, they can also show specific geographic features such as roads, mountains, and rivers. They can also show information according to geographic distribution such as population, housing, or manufacturing centers.

- **Illustrations**
  A wide range of illustrations, such as pictures, drawings, and diagrams, may be used to illuminate the text in a document. They may also be a part of a graphic layout designed to make the page more attractive.

To make a **bar graph** or a **pictograph**, determine the scale to be used for the graph. Then determine the length of each bar on the graph or determine the number of pictures needed to represent each item of information. Be sure to include an explanation of the scale in the legend.

Example: A class had the following grades:
4 A's, 9 B's, 8 C's, 1 D, 3 F's
Graph these on a pictograph and a bar graph.

Pictograph

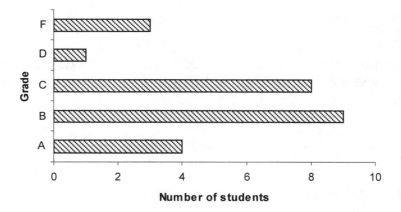

Grade	Number of Students
A	☺☺☺☺
B	☺☺☺☺☺☺☺☺☺
C	☺☺☺☺☺☺☺☺
D	☺
F	☺☺☺

Bar graph

To make a **line graph**, determine appropriate scales for both the vertical and horizontal axes (based on the information to be graphed). Describe what each axis represents, and mark the scale periodically on each axis. Graph the individual points of the graph, and connect the points on the graph from left to right.

Example: Graph the following information using a line graph.

The number of National Merit finalists/school year

	90–91	91–92	92–93	93–94	94–95	95–96
Central	3	5	1	4	6	8
Wilson	4	2	3	2	3	2

To make a **circle graph**, total all the information that is to be included on the graph. Determine the central angle to be used for each sector of the graph using the following formula:

$$\frac{\text{information}}{\text{total information}} \times 360° = \text{degrees in central } \square$$

Lay out the central angles to these sizes, and label each section and include its percent.

Example: Graph this information on a circle graph:

Monthly expenses:

       Rent, $400
       Food, $150
       Utilities, $75
       Clothes, $75
       Church, $100
       Misc., $200

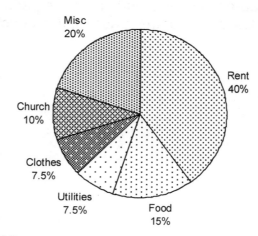

Scatter plots compare two characteristics of the same group of things or people and usually consist of a large body of data. They show how much one variable is affected by another. The relationship between the two variables is their **correlation**. The closer the data points come to making a straight line when plotted, the closer the correlation.

Stem-and-leaf plots are visually similar to line plots. The **stems** are the digits in the greatest place value of the data values, and the **leaves** are the digits in the next greatest place values. Stem-and-leaf plots are best suited for small sets of data and are especially useful for comparing two sets of data. The following is an example using test scores:

4	9
5	4 9
6	1 2 3 4 6 7 8 8
7	0 3 4 6 6 6 7 7 7 8 8 8 8
8	3 5 5 7 8
9	0 0 3 4 5
10	0 0

Histograms are used to summarize information from large sets of data that can be naturally grouped into intervals. The vertical axis indicates **frequency** (the number of times any particular data value occurs), and the horizontal axis indicates data values or ranges of data values. The number of data values in any interval is the **frequency of the interval**.

DOMAIN II WRITING KNOWLEDGE AND PROFICIENCY

COMPETENCY 6.0 **UNDERSTAND THE INFLUENCE OF PURPOSE AND AUDIENCE IN WRITTEN COMMUNICATION.**

Skill 6.1 **Identify written material consistent with a specific purpose or audience (e.g., a business letter, a speech to a skeptical audience).**

Because students typically write for their instructor, they have a narrow view of audience. They must learn to adapt their communication to the needs of their audiences. One way to teach this is to have students determine the values, needs, constraints, and demographics of their audience.

Values: What is important to this group of people? What is their background and how will that affect their perception of your speech?

Needs: Find out in advance what the audience's needs are. Why are they listening to you? Find a way to satisfy their needs.

Constraints: What might hold the audience back from being fully engaged in what you are saying, or agreeing with your point of view, or processing what you are trying to say? These could be political reasons, which make them wary of your presentation's ideology from the start, or knowledge reasons, in which the audience lacks the appropriate background information to grasp your ideas. Avoid this last constraint by staying away from technical terminology, slang, or abbreviations that may be unclear to your audience.

Demographic Information: Take the audience's size into account as well as the location of the presentation. Demographics could include age, gender, education, religion, income level and other such countable characteristics.

Start where the listeners are, and then take them where you want to go!

Just as you talk to different people in different ways so do you write in different styles and levels of formality. Students should learn that writers use different writing styles to accomplish their purposes and to reach their different audiences.

Is a **business letter** outdated? Although much business-letter writing has been relegated to e-mail communications, letters are still a valuable form of communication. A carefully written letter can be powerful. It can convince, persuade, entice, motivate, and/or create good will.

As with any other communication, you will need to know information about your receiver. This may be complicated if there will be more than one receiver of the message; in these cases, write for the largest or most important group of readers without "writing down" to any of those who will read and be affected or influenced by the letter. It may be better to send more than one form of the letter to the various receivers in some cases.

Purpose is the most powerful factor in writing a business letter. What is the letter expected to accomplish? Is it intended to motivate the receiver to act or to act in a specific manner? Are you hoping to see some action take place as the result of the letter? If so, you should clearly define for yourself what the purpose is before you craft the letter. To avoid procrastination, include a time deadline for the response.

Why should you choose a letter format as your channel of communication?

1. It's easy to keep a record of the transaction.
2. The message can be edited and perfected before it is transmitted.
3. It facilitates the handling of details.
4. It's ideal for communicating complex information.
5. It's a good way to disseminate mass messages at a relatively low cost.

Because letters have external readers, they typically use formal language. They should be straightforward and courteous. The writing should be concise and complete; otherwise, more than one exchange of letters or phone calls to get the message across may be necessary.

A **complaint** is a different kind of business letter. It can come under the classification of a "bad news" business letter, and guidelines are helpful when writing this kind of letter. A positive writing style can overcome much of the inherent negativity of a letter of complaint. No matter how much in the right you may be, maintaining self-control and courtesy and avoiding demeaning or blaming language is more likely to be effective. Abruptness, condescension, or harshness of tone will not help achieve your purpose, particularly if you are requesting a positive response such as reimbursement for a bad product or some help in righting a wrong that may have been done to you. The goal is to solve the specific problem and to retain the good will of the receiver if possible.

Induction is better than deduction for this type of communication. Beginning with the details and building to the statement of the problem generally has the effect of softening the bad news. It's also useful to begin with an opening that will serve as a buffer. The same is true for the closing. Leave the reader with a favorable impression by writing a closing paragraph that will generate good will rather than bad.

E-mail has revolutionized business communications. It has most of the advantages of business letters and the added ones of immediacy, lower costs, and convenience. Even very long reports can be attached to an e-mail. On the other hand, a two-line message can be sent and a response received immediately bringing together the features of a postal system and the telephone.

Instant messaging goes even one step further. It can do all of the above—send messages, attach reports—and still have many of the advantages of a telephone conversation. E-mail has an unwritten code of behavior that includes restrictions on how informal the writing can be. The level of accepted business conversation is usually also acceptable in e-mails. Capital letters and bolding are considered shouting and are usually frowned on.

Remind students that e-mail messages, even if intended for just one reader, may eventually reach a much wider audience. In recent years, a number of e-mail writers have found themselves in embarrassing situations or legal troubles because of the circulation of their personal e-mails on the Internet. When writers need to address a sensitive, unpleasant or controversial matter, they should consult state laws to determine whether personal privacy laws protect correspondence. If the law does protect such correspondence from being circulated by the addressee, then the writers may wish to mention this in their messages to forestall publication. Otherwise, clarity, concision, and civility in written works will protect writers.

Personal Letters

When writing personal notes or letters, the writer needs to keep the following key matters in mind:

- Once the topic is determined, the writer must determine the appropriate tone to introduce and express it. Is humor appropriate? Seriousness? Bluntness or subtlety? Does the situation call for formal or informal language? The answers to these questions will depend, in good part, on the writer's relationship to the reader. Plan appropriately regarding situation and audience.
- Does the writer's introduction clearly explain the topic/situation to a reader who doesn't know or feel what the reader knows or feels? Don't assume that the writer and reader are of the same mindset. Use a checklist to make sure all key information is clearly and concisely expressed.
- If a note or letter involves a request, what type of response/result does the writer desire? Devise a strategy or strategies for achieving a desired outcome.
- If a note or letter involves a complaint about the reader, the writer will need to decide whether to ask for particular amends or to let the reader decide what, if anything, to do. If no amends are requested, the writer may wish to suggest ideas that would help to avoid similar conflicts in the future. Asking the reader for his or her opinions is also a possibility.

- If a timely response to any note or letter is needed, the writer must mention this.

Provide students in-class opportunities to write a variety of personal notes and letters, whether involving real life or hypothetical situations. Invitations, thank-you notes, complaints, requests for favors, or personal updates are a few of the options available. Have students experiment with a variety of tones and strategies on a particular piece of personal correspondence. For example, they could write a complaint letter in a blunt tone, then write the same complaint in a humorous tone; compare and contrast the drafts. Structure in-class activities to allow for peer feedback.

Types of Persuasive Speech

1. **Fact**: Similar to an informative speech, a persuasive speech on a question of fact seeks to find an answer where there isn't a clear one. The speaker evaluates evidence and attempts to convince the audience that their conclusion is correct. The challenge is to accept a certain carefully crafted view of the facts presented.

2. **Value**: This kind of persuasion tries to convince the audience that a certain thing is good or bad, moral or immoral, valuable or worthless. It focuses less on knowledge and more on beliefs and values.

3. **Policy**: This speech is a call to action, arguing that something should be done, improved, or changed. Its goal is action from the audience, but it also seeks passive agreement with the proposition proposed. It appeals to both reason and emotion, and tells listeners what they can do and how to do it.

Skill 6.2   Adapt writing (e.g., in terms of sentence structure or vocabulary) for different purposes or audiences.

Tailoring language for a particular **audience** is an important skill. Writing to be read by a business associate will surely sound different from writing to be read by a younger sibling. Not only are the vocabularies different, but the formality/informality of the discourse will also need to be adjusted.

Determining what the language should be for a particular audience, then, hinges on two things: **word choice** and **formality/informality**. The most formal language does not use contractions or slang. The most informal language will probably feature a more casual use of common sayings and anecdotes. Formal language will use longer sentences and will not sound like a conversation. The most informal language will use shorter sentences—not necessarily simple sentences, but shorter constructions—and may sound like a conversation.

In both formal and informal writing, there exists a **tone**, the writer's attitude toward the material and/or readers. Tone may be playful, formal, intimate, angry, serious, ironic, outraged, baffled, tender, serene, depressed, and so on. Both the subject matter and the audience dictate the overall tone of a piece of writing. Tone is also related to the actual words that make up the document, as we attach affective meanings to words, called **connotations**. Gaining this conscious control over language makes it possible to use language appropriately in various situations and to evaluate its uses in literature and other forms of communication. By evoking the proper responses from readers/listeners, we can prompt them to take action.

The following questions are an excellent way to assess the audience and tone of a given piece of writing.

1. Who is your audience? (friend, teacher, business person, someone else)
2. How much does this person know about you and/or your topic?
3. What is your purpose? (to prove an argument, to persuade, to amuse, to register a complaint, to ask for a raise, etc.)
4. What emotions do you have about the topic? (nervous, happy, confident, angry, sad, no feelings at all)
5. What emotions do you want to register with your audience? (anger, nervousness, happiness, boredom, interest)
6. What persona do you need to create in order to achieve your purpose?
7. What choice of language is best suited to achieving your purpose with your particular subject? (slang, friendly but respectful, formal)
8. What emotional quality do you want to transmit to achieve your purpose (matter of fact, informative, authoritative, inquisitive, sympathetic, or angry) and to what degree do you want to express this tone?

COMPETENCY 7.0   APPLY PRINCIPLES OF UNITY, FOCUS, AND DEVELOPMENT IN WRITING.

Skill 7.1   Recognize examples of well-developed writing.

Through critical analysis, you can recognize a piece of writing that is unified, coherent, and well developed. To achieve unity, the writer will ensure that all parts work together to develop the thesis. Even the smallest detail can serve a purpose, such as developing the mood or setting the appropriate tone. To achieve coherence, the writer will use a structure that focuses on the main idea. In some cases, a transitional word or sentence will clarify the relationship of the ideas. For example, the author uses "because" to indicate cause and effect. This approach is more subtle than a direct announcement that Point A caused Point B. To achieve complete development, the author will strive for balance, providing the reader with sufficient and appropriate detail.

Here's a piece of writing that exemplifies these principles. Notice how the essay writer identifies the ways that the structure of the writing helps to develop the theme.

Sample Prompt and Well-Written Response:

Written on July 15, 1944, three weeks before the Nazis arrested the Frank family, Anne's diary entry explains her worldview and future hopes.

> *It's difficult in times like these: ideals, dreams, and cherished hopes rise within us, only to be crushed by grim reality. It's a wonder I haven't abandoned all my ideals; they seem so absurd and impractical. Yet I cling to them because I still believe, in spite of everything, that people are truly good at heart.*

> *It's utterly impossible for me to build my life on a foundation of chaos, suffering, and death. I see the world being slowly transformed into a wilderness, I hear the approaching thunder that, one day, will destroy us too, I feel the suffering of millions, and yet, when I look up at the sky, I somehow feel that everything will change for the better, that this cruelty too shall end, that peace and tranquility will return once more. In the meantime, I must hold on to my ideals. Perhaps the day will come when I will be able to realize them!*

Using your knowledge of literature, write a response in which you:

- Compare and contrast Anne's ideals with her awareness of the conditions in which she lives; and
- Discuss how the structure of Anne's writing—her sentences and paragraphs—emphasize the above contrast.

Sample Response

This excerpt from The Diary of Anne Frank reveals the inner strength of a young girl who refuses, despite the wartime violence and danger surrounding her, to let her idealism be overcome by hatred and mass killing. This idealism is reflected, in part, by her emphases on universal human hopes, such as peace, tranquility, and goodwill. However, Anne Frank is no dreamy Pollyanna. Reflecting on her idealism in the context of the war raging around her, she matter-of-factly writes, "My dreams, they seem so absurd and impractical."

This indicates Anne Frank's awareness of not only her own predicament, but of human miseries that extend beyond the immediate circumstances of her life. For elsewhere, she writes in a similar vein, "In times like these... I see the world being slowly transformed into a wilderness"; despite her own suffering, she can "feel the suffering of millions."

Yet Anne Frank believes, "in spite of everything, that people are truly good at heart." This statement epitomizes the stark existential contrast of her worldview with the wartime reality that ultimately claimed her life.

The statement also exemplifies how Anne's literary form—her syntax and diction—mirror thematic content and contrasts. "In spite of everything," she still believes in people. She can "hear the approaching thunder...yet, when I look up at the sky, I somehow feel that everything will change for the better." At numerous points in this diary entry, first-hand knowledge of violent tragedy stands side-by-side with belief in humanity and human progress.

"I must hold on to my ideals," Anne concludes. "Perhaps the day will come when I'll be able to realize them!" In her diary, she has done so, and more.

Skill 7.2   Make revisions that improve the unity and focus of a paragraph or passage.

Unity

Usually, prose that lacks unity fails for one of the following reasons: (1) it lacks a clear statement of a main idea; (2) the opening statement misdirects the reader because it makes a commitment that the writing does not—perhaps cannot—meet; (3) subdivisions are not so selected or phrased that they clarify their relation to the main idea.

A good topic statement works for the writer because it appropriately directs the writer's commitment. A topic sentence is only effective if the details that follow develop it and firm it up.

- The details may cite particulars, instances, examples, and illustrations. Probably the easiest way to clarify a topic sentence is to provide instances.

- On the other hand, an incident or extended illustration can also be used effectively. The writer may establish the topic sentence by telling a story or describing a single illustration in some detail. This extended illustration might be an analogy.

- Yet another way to develop a topic sentence is by using cause-and-effect speculations.

- Comparison and contrast are often used very effectively in establishing a point. It is like this, but not like that.

- Not used as often, but still a viable alternative, is a restatement and amplification of the topic sentence itself.

Focus

Point of view defines the focus a writer assumes in relation to a given topic. It is extremely important to maintain a consistent point of view in order to create coherent paragraphs. Point of view is related to matters of person, tense, tone, and number.

Person—A shift in the form that indicates whether a person is speaking (first), is being spoken to (second), or is being spoken about (third) can disrupt continuity of a passage. In your essay, it is recommended that you write in the third person, as it is often considered the most formal of the modes of person. If you do decide to use the more informal first or second person (I, you, or we) in your essay, be careful not to shift between first, second, and third persons from sentence to sentence or paragraph to paragraph.

Tense—Verb tenses indicate the time of an action or state of being—the past, present, or future. It is important to stick largely to a selected tense, though this may not always be the case. For instance, in an essay about the history of environmental protection, it might be necessary to include a paragraph about the future benefits or consequences of protecting the earth.

Tone—The tone of an essay varies greatly with the purpose, subject, and audience

Number—Words change when their meanings are singular or plural. Make sure that you do not shift number needlessly; if a meaning is singular in one sentence, do not make it plural in the subsequent sentence.

Techniques for revising written texts to achieve clarity and economy of expression

Enhancing Interest:

- Start out with an attention-grabbing introduction. This sets an engaging tone for the entire piece, and it will be more likely to pull in the reader.
- Use dynamic vocabulary and varied sentence beginnings. Keep the readers on their toes. If they can predict what you are going to say next, switch it up.
- Avoid using clichés (e.g., as cold as ice, the best thing since sliced bread, nip it in the bud). These are easy shortcuts, but they are not interesting, memorable, or convincing.

Ensuring Understanding:

- Avoid using the words, "clearly," "obviously," and "undoubtedly." Often, things that are clear or obvious to the author are not as apparent to the reader. Instead of using these words, make your point so strongly that it is clear on its own.
- Use the word that best fits the meaning you intend, even if it is longer or a little less common. Try to find a balance, and go with a familiar yet precise word.
- When in doubt, explain further.

Skill 7.3   Identify information, statements, or details presented in a paragraph or passage that are off topic.

Techniques to Maintain Focus

- **Focus on a main point.** The point should be clear to readers, and all sentences in the paragraph should relate to it.

- **Start the paragraph with a topic sentence.** This should be a general, one-sentence summary of the paragraph's main point, relating both back towards the thesis and toward the content of the paragraph. (A topic sentence is sometimes unnecessary if the paragraph continues a developing idea clearly introduced in a preceding paragraph, or if the paragraph appears in a narrative of events, where generalizations might interrupt the flow of the story.)

- **Stick to the point.** Eliminate sentences that do not support the topic sentence.

- **Be flexible.** If there is not enough evidence to support the claim your topic sentence is making, do not fall into the trap of wandering or introducing new ideas within the paragraph. Either find more evidence, or adjust the topic sentence to collaborate with the available evidence.

The following passage has several irrelevant sentences that are highlighted in bold.

> The New City Planning Committee is proposing a new capitol building to represent the multicultural face of New City. **The current mayor is a Democrat.** The new capitol building will be on 10th Street across from the grocery store and next to the Recreational Center. It will be within walking distance to the subway and bus depot, as the designers want to emphasize the importance of public transportation. Aesthetically, the building will have a contemporary design, featuring a brushed-steel exterior and large, floor-to-ceiling windows. **It is important for employees to have a connection with the outside world even when they are in their offices.** Inside the building, the walls will be moveable. This will not only facilitate a multitude of creative floor plans, but it will also create a focus on open communication and flow of information. **It sounds a bit gimmicky to me.** Finally, the capitol will feature a large outdoor courtyard full of lush greenery and serene fountains. **Work will now seem like Club Med to those who work at the New City capitol!**

Skill 7.4   Select supporting material consistent with the argument or main idea of a paragraph or passage.

Effective argumentative discourse is based on the strengths of the writer's support. Using reliable and relevant facts, an argument can convince or motivate.

An argument is a generalization that is proven or supported with facts. If the facts are not accurate, the generalization remains unproven. Using inaccurate "facts" to support an argument is called a *fallacy* in reasoning.

Accuracy

Some factors to consider in judging whether the facts used to support an argument are accurate are as follow:

- Are the facts current or are they out of date? For example, if the proposition "birth defects in babies born to drug-using mothers are increasing," then the data must include the latest that is available.

- Another important factor to consider in judging the accuracy of a fact is its source. Where was the data obtained, and is that source reliable?

- The calculations on which the facts are based may be unreliable. Before using a piece of derived information, can you repeat the results by making your own calculations?

Relevance

Even facts that are true and have a sharp impact on the argument may not be relevant to the case at hand.

- Health statistics from an entire state may have no relevance, or little relevance, to a particular county or zip code. Statistics from an entire country cannot be used to prove very much about a particular state or county.

- An analogy can be useful in making a point, but the comparison must match up in all characteristics or it will not be relevant. Analogy should be used very carefully. It is often just as likely to destroy an argument as it is to strengthen it.

Importance

The importance or significance of a fact may not strengthen an argument. For example, of the millions of immigrants in the U.S., using a single family to support a solution to the immigration problem will not make much difference overall even though those single-example arguments are often used to support one approach or another. They may achieve a positive reaction, but they will not prove that one solution is better than another. If enough cases were cited from a variety of geographical locations, the information might be significant.

Sufficiency

How much is enough? Generally speaking, three strong supporting facts are sufficient to establish the thesis of an argument. For example:

Conclusion: All green apples are sour.

- When I was a child, I bit into a green apple from my grandfather's orchard, and it was sour.
- I once bought green apples from a roadside vendor, and when I bit into one, it was sour.
- My grocery store had a sale on green Granny Smith apples last week, and I bought several only to find that they were sour when I bit into one.

The fallacy in the above argument is that the sample was insufficient. A more exhaustive search of literature will probably turn up some green apples that are not sour.

Sometimes more than three arguments are too many. On the other hand, it's not unusual to hear public speakers, particularly politicians, who will cite a long litany of facts to support their positions.

A very good example of the omission of facts in an argument is the résumé of an applicant for a job. The applicant is arguing that he or she should be awarded a particular job. The application form will ask for information about past employment, and unfavorable dismissals from jobs in the past may just be omitted. Employers are usually suspicious of periods of time when the applicant has not listed an employer.

A writer makes choices about which facts will be used and which will be discarded in developing an argument. Those choices may exclude anything that is not supportive of the point of view the arguer is taking. It's always a good idea for the reader to do some research to spot the omissions and to ask whether they have an impact on the acceptance of the point of view presented in the argument.

No judgment is either black or white. If the argument seems too neat or too compelling, there are probably facts that might be relevant that have not been included.

COMPETENCY 8.0   APPLY PRINCIPLES OF ORGANIZATION IN WRITING.

Skill 8.1   Recognize effective organization in a written passage.

The **organization** of a written work includes two factors: the order in which the writer has chosen to present the different parts of the discussion or argument and the relationships he or she constructs between these parts.

Written ideas need to be presented in a **logical order** so that a reader can follow the information easily and quickly. There are many different ways in which to order a series of ideas, but they all share one thing—to lead the reader along a desired path, while avoiding backtracking and skipping around, in order to give a clear, strong presentation of the writer's main idea. The following are *some* of the ways in which a paragraph may be organized.

Sequence of events—In this type of organization, the details are presented in the order in which they have occurred. Paragraphs that describe a process or procedure, give directions, or outline a given period (such as a day or a month) are often arranged chronologically.

Statement support—In this type of organization, the main idea is stated, and the rest of the paragraph explains or proves it. This is also referred to as relative or order of importance. This type of order is organized in four ways: most to least, least to most, most least most, and least most least.

Comparison-Contrast—The compare-contrast pattern is used when a paragraph describes the differences or similarities of two or more ideas, actions, events, or things. Usually, the topic sentence describes the basic relationship between the ideas or items, and the rest of the paragraph explains this relationship.

Classification—In this type of organization, the paragraph presents grouped information about a topic. The topic sentence usually states the general category, and the rest of the sentences show how various elements of the category have a common base and how they differ from the common base.

Cause-and-Effect—This pattern describes how two or more events are connected. The main sentence usually states the primary cause(s) and the primary effect(s), and their basic connection. The rest of the sentences explain the connection—how one event caused the next.

Spatial/Place—In this type of organization, certain descriptions are organized according to the location of items in relation to each other and to a larger context. The orderly arrangement guides the reader's eye as he or she mentally envisions the scene or place being described.

Example, Clarification, and Definition—These types of organizations show, explain, or elaborate on the main idea. This can be done by showing specific cases, examining meaning multiple times, or describing one term extensively.

Skill 8.2   Reorganize sentences or paragraphs to achieve an effective sequence of ideas.

Paragraphs should contain concrete, interesting information and supporting details to support the main idea or point of view. Fact statements add weight to opinions, especially when the writer is trying to convince the reader of his or her viewpoint. Because every good thesis has an assertion, a well-written passage offers specifics, facts, data, anecdotes, expert opinion, and other details to *show* or *prove* that assertion. While *the author* knows what he or she wants to convey, the *reader* does not.

Like a whole piece of writing, the paragraphs that make up that piece can take a number of forms or combinations of forms. These forms help create an organized and well-structured document:

Cause-and-effect is used to show the reasons for the result of some action.

Compare-and-contrast is used to show similarities and differences between two or more items.

Definition is used if a simple dictionary definition is not sufficient.

Example and illustration is used to show a point by citing examples.

Sequence and process is used to show a step-by-step procedure.

A piece of writing should end with a brief straightforward **concluding paragraph** that ties together the written content and leaves the reader with a sense of its completion. The conclusion should reinforce the main points and offer some insight into the topic, provide a sense of unity for the essay by relating it to the thesis, and signal clear closure of the essay.

Skill 8.3 **Identify appropriate transitional words or phrases (e.g., "however," "as a result," "moreover") to help readers understand the organization of ideas.**

Even if the sentences that make up a given paragraph or passage are arranged in logical order, the document as a whole can still seem choppy, the various ideas disconnected. **Transitions**, words that signal relationships between ideas, can help improve the flow of a document. Transitions can help achieve clear and effective presentation of information by establishing connections between sentences, paragraphs, and sections of a document. With transitions, each sentence builds on the ideas in the last, and each paragraph has clear links to the preceding one. As a result, the reader receives clear directions on how to piece together the writer's ideas in a logically coherent argument. By signaling how to organize, interpret, and react to information, transitions allow a writer to explain his or her ideas effectively and elegantly.

Logical Relationship	Transitional Expression
Similarity	also, in the same way, just as ... so too, likewise, similarly
Exception/Contrast	but, however, in spite of, on the one hand ... on the other hand, nevertheless, nonetheless, notwithstanding, in contrast, on the contrary, still, yet
Sequence/Order	first, second, third, ... next, then, finally
Time	after, afterward, at last, before, currently, during, earlier, immediately, later, meanwhile, now, recently, simultaneously, subsequently, then
Example	for example, for instance, namely, specifically, to illustrate
Emphasis	even, indeed, in fact, of course, truly
Place/Position	above, adjacent, below, beyond, here, in front, in back, nearby, there
Cause and Effect	accordingly, consequently, hence, so, therefore, thus
Additional Support or Evidence	additionally, again, also, and, as well, besides, equally important, further, furthermore, in addition, moreover, then
Conclusion/Summary	finally, in a word, in brief, in conclusion, in the end, in the final analysis, on the whole, thus, to conclude, to summarize, in sum, in summary

The following example shows good logical order and transitions, with the transition words being highlighted.

No one really knows how Valentine's Day started. There are several legends, **however**, which are often told. The **first** attributes Valentine's Day to a Christian priest who lived in Rome during the third century, under the rule of Emperor Claudius. Rome was at war, and **apparently,** Claudius felt that married men did not fight as well as bachelors. **Consequently**, Claudius banned marriage for the duration of the war. **However,** Valentinus, the priest, risked his life to marry couples secretly in violation of Claudius' law. The **second** legend is **even more** romantic. **In this story**, Valentinus is a prisoner, having been condemned to death for refusing to worship pagan deities. **While** in jail, he fell in love with his jailer's daughter, who happened to be blind. Daily, he prayed for her sight to return, and miraculously it did. On February 14, the day that he was condemned to die, he was allowed to write the young woman a note. **In this farewell letter**, he promised eternal love, and signed at the bottom of the page the now famous words, "Your Valentine."

COMPETENCY 9.0   **APPLY PRINCIPLES OF SENTENCE AND PARAGRAPH CONSTRUCTION IN WRITING.**

Skill 9.1   Recognize effective topic sentences.

Topic Sentences

Just as the essay must have an overall focus reflected in the thesis statement, each paragraph must have a central idea reflected in the topic sentence. A good topic sentence also provides transition from the previous paragraph and relates to the essay's thesis. Good topic sentences, therefore, provide unity throughout the essay.

Consider the following potential topic sentences. Be sure that each provides transition and clearly states the subject of the paragraph.

Topic Sentence 1: *Computers are used in science.*

Analysis: This sentence simply states the topic—computers used in science. It does not relate to the thesis or provide transition from the introduction. The reader still does not know how computers are used.

Topic Sentence 2: *Now I will talk about computers used in science.*

Analysis: Like the faulty "announcer" thesis statement, this "announcer" topic sentence is vague and merely names the topic.

Topic Sentence 3: *First, computers used in science have improved our lives.*

Analysis: The transition word *First* helps link the introduction and this paragraph. It adds unity to the essay. It, however, does not give specifics about the improvement computers have made in our lives.

Topic Sentence 4: *First used in scientific research and spaceflights, computers are now used extensively in the diagnosis and treatment of disease.*

Analysis: This sentence is the most thorough and fluent. It provides specific areas that will be discussed in the paragraph and it offers more than an announcement of the topic. The writer gives concrete information about the content of the paragraph that will follow.

Summary Guidelines for Writing Topic Sentences
1. Specifically relate the topic to the thesis statement.
2. State clearly and concretely the subject of the paragraph.
3. Provide some transition from the previous paragraph.
4. Avoid topic sentences that are facts, questions, or announcers.

Skill 9.2   Recognize wordiness and redundancy in sentences and paragraphs.

Revision of sentences to eliminate wordiness, ambiguity, and redundancy

Sometimes students see this exercise as simply catching errors in spelling or word use. Students need to reframe their thinking about revising and editing. Some questions that need to be asked include:

- Is the reasoning coherent?
- Is the point established?
- Does the introduction make the reader want to read this discourse?
- What is the thesis? Is it proven?
- What is the purpose? Is it clear? Is it useful, valuable, and interesting?
- Is the style of writing so wordy that it exhausts the reader and interferes with engagement?
- Is the writing so spare that it is boring?
- Are the sentences too uniform in structure?
- Are there too many simple sentences?
- Are too many of the complex sentences the same structure?
- Are the compounds truly compounds, or are they unbalanced?
- Are parallel structures truly parallel?
- If there are characters, are they believable?
- If there is dialogue, is it natural or stilted?
- Is the title appropriate?
- Does the writing show creativity, or is it boring?
- Is the language appropriate? Is it too formal? Too informal? If jargon is used, is it appropriate?

Studies have clearly demonstrated that the most fertile area in teaching writing is this one. If students can learn to revise their own work effectively, they are well on their way to becoming effective, mature writers. Word processing is an important tool for teaching this stage in the writing process. Microsoft Word has tracking features that make the revision exchanges between teachers and students more effective than ever before.

Skill 9.3   Identify sentence fragments and run-on sentences.

Fragments

Fragments occur (1) if word groups standing alone are missing either a subject or a verb, or (2) if word groups containing a subject and verb and standing alone are actually made dependent because of the use of subordinating conjunctions or relative pronouns.

Error: The teacher waiting for the class to complete the assignment.

Problem: This sentence is not complete because an *-ing* word alone does not function as a verb. When a helping verb is added (for example, *was*), it will become a sentence.

Correction: *The teacher was waiting for the class to complete the assignment.*

Error: Until the last toy was removed from the floor.

Problem: Words such as until, because, although, when, and if make a clause dependent and thus incapable of standing alone. An independent clause must be added to make the sentence complete.

Correction: *Until the last toy was removed from the floor, the kids could not go outside to play.*

Error: The city will close the public library. Because of a shortage of funds.

Problem: The problem is the same as above. The dependent clause must be joined to the independent clause.

Correction: *The city will close the public library because of a shortage of funds.*

Error: Anyone planning to go on the trip should bring the necessary items. Such as a backpack, boots, a canteen, and bug spray.

Problem: The second word group is a phrase and cannot stand alone because there is neither a subject nor a verb. The fragment can be corrected by adding the phrase to the sentence.

Correction: *Anyone planning to go on the trip should bring the necessary items, such as a backpack, boots, a canteen, and bug spray.*

Fragments are tested in sentences tied to a passage. Items will be in one of two formats.

FORMAT A

Forensics experts conclude that the residents died from chemical <u>radiation. Or</u> perhaps from a mixture of toxic substances and asphyxiation.

A) radiation; or
B) radiation or
C) radiation or,
D) No change is necessary

FORMAT B

<u>Forensics</u> experts conclude that the residents died from chemical <u>radiation. Or</u> perhaps from a mixture of toxic substances and <u>asphyxiation</u>.

A) Forensics
B) radiation or
C) asphyxiation
D) No change is necessary

In each case, you must consider the punctuation between *radiation* and *or*. The punctuation decision is difficult if you do not understand that the second group of words, the one that begins with *Or*, is not a sentence. While these questions may appear to be only about punctuation, they are also about fragments.

The answer in both formats is B. The word group *"Or perhaps from a mixture of toxic substances and asphyxiation"* lacks a subject and a complete verb. It must be joined to the preceding sentence. A comma is not necessary since the word *residents* is the subject of the verb phrase *"died from chemical radiation and of asphyxiation."*

PRACTICE EXERCISE—FRAGMENTS

Choose the option that corrects the underlined portion(s) of the sentence.
If no error exists, choose "No change is necessary."

1. Despite the lack of funds in the <u>budget it</u> was necessary to rebuild the roads that were damaged from the recent floods.

   A. budget: it
   B. budget, it
   C. budget; it
   D. No change is necessary

2. After determining that the fire was caused by faulty <u>wiring, the</u> building inspector said the construction company should be fined.

   A. wiring. The
   B. wiring the
   C. wiring; the
   D. No change is necessary

3. Computers are being used more and more <u>frequently. because</u> of their capacity to store information.

   A. frequently because
   B. frequently, because
   C. frequently; because
   D. No change is necessary

4. Doug washed the floors <u>every day. to</u> keep them clean for the guests.

   A. every day to
   B. every day,
   C. every day;
   D. No change is necessary.

ANSWER KEY: PRACTICE EXERCISE FOR FRAGMENTS

1. The correct answer is B. The clause that begins with *despite* is independent and must be separated with the clause that follows by a comma. Option A is incorrect because a colon is used to set off a list or to emphasize what follows. In Option B, a comma incorrectly suggests that the two clauses are dependent.

2. The correct answer is D. In the test item, a comma correctly separates the dependent clause *After...wiring* at the beginning of the sentence from the independent clause that follows. Option A incorrectly breaks the two clauses into separate sentences, while Option B omits the comma, and Option C incorrectly suggests that the phrase is an independent clause.

3. The correct answer is A. The second clause *because...information* is dependent and must be joined to the first independent clause. Option B is incorrect because as the dependent clause comes at the end of the sentence, rather than at the beginning, a comma is not necessary. In Option C, a semi-colon incorrectly suggests that the two clauses are independent.

4. The correct answer is A. The second clause *to keep...guests* is dependent and must be joined to the first independent clause. Option B is incorrect because as the dependent clause comes at the end of the sentence, rather than at the beginning, a comma is not necessary. In Option C, a semi-colon incorrectly suggests that the two clauses are independent.

Run-on sentences and comma splices

Comma splices appear when only a comma joins two sentences. Fused sentences appear when two sentences are run together with no punctuation at all.

Error: Dr. Sanders is a brilliant scientist, his research on genetic disorders won him a Nobel Prize.

Problem: A comma alone cannot join two independent clauses (complete sentences). The two clauses can be joined by a semi-colon or they can be separated by a period.

Correction: *Dr. Sanders is a brilliant scientist; his research on genetic disorders won him a Nobel Prize.*
                            -OR-
                Dr. Sanders is a brilliant scientist. His research on genetic disorders won him a Nobel Prize.

Error: Florida is noted for its beaches they are long, sandy, and beautiful.

Problem: The first sentence ends with the word beaches, and the second sentence cannot be joined with the first. The fused sentence error can be corrected in a few ways: (1) one clause may be made dependent on another with a subordinating conjunction or a relative pronoun, (2) a semi-colon may be used to combine two equally important ideas, or (3) the two independent clauses may be separated by a period.

Correction: *Florida is noted for its beaches, which are long, sandy, and beautiful.*

-OR-

Florida is noted for its beaches; they are long, sandy, and beautiful.

-OR-

Florida is noted for its beaches. They are long, sandy, and beautiful.

Error: The number of hotels has increased, however, the number of visitors has grown also.

Problem: The first sentence ends with the word increased, and a comma is not strong enough to connect it to the second sentence. The adverbial transition *however* does not function the same way as a coordinating conjunction and cannot be used with commas to link two sentences. Several different corrections are available.

Correction: *The number of hotels has increased; however, the number of visitors has grown also.*

[Two separate but closely related sentences are created with the use of the semicolon.]

-OR-

The number of hotels has increased. However, the number of visitors has grown also.

[Two separate sentences are created.]

-OR-

Although the number of hotels has increased, the number of visitors has grown also.

[One idea is made subordinate to the other and separated with a comma.]

-OR-

The number of hotels has increased, but the number of visitors has grown also.

[The comma before the coordinating conjunction *but* is appropriate. The adverbial transition *however* does not function the same way as the coordinating conjunction *but* does.]

PRACTICE EXERCISE—FUSED SENTENCES AND COMMA SPLICES

Choose the option that corrects an error in the underlined portion(s). Ifno error exists, choose "No change is necessary."

1. Scientists are excited at the ability to clone a <u>sheep; however,</u> it is not yet known if the same can be done to humans.

    A.   sheep, however,
    B.   sheep. However,
    C.   sheep, however;
    D.   No change is necessary

2. Because of the rising cost of college tuition the federal government now offers special financial assistance, such as loans, to students.

    A.   tuition, the
    B.   tuition; the
    C.   such as loans
    D.   No change is necessary

3. As the number of homeless people continue to rise, the major cities like New York and Chicago, are now investing millions of dollars in low-income housing.

    A.   rise. The major cities
    B.   rise; the major cities
    C.   New York and Chicago
    D.   No change is necessary

4. Unlike in the 1950's, most households find the husband and wife in many different career fields working full-time to make ends meet.

    A.   the 1950's; most
    B.   the 1950's most
    C.   ends meet, in many
    D.   No change is necessary

ANSWER KEY: PRACTICE EXERCISE FOR COMMA SPLICES AND FUSED SENTENCES

1. Option B correctly separates two independent clauses. The comma in Option A after the word sheep creates a run-on sentence. The semi-colon in Option C does separate the two clauses but occurs at an inappropriate point.

2. The comma in Option A correctly separates the independent clause and the dependent clause. The semi-colon in Option B is incorrect because one of the clauses is independent. Option C requires a comma to prevent a run-on sentence.

3. Option C is correct because a comma creates a run-on. Option A is incorrect because the first clause is dependent. The semi-colon in Option B incorrectly divides the dependent clause from the independent clause.

4. Option D correctly separates the two clauses with a comma. Option A incorrectly uses a semi-colon to divide the clauses. The lack of a comma in Option B creates a run-on sentence Option C puts a comma in an inappropriate place.

COMPETENCY 10.0   **APPLY CORRECT USAGE IN STANDARD ENGLISH.**

Skill 10.1   **Recognize the standard use of verbs (e.g., subject-verb agreement, verb tense).**

A verb must correspond in the singular or plural form with the simple subject; it is not affected by any interfering elements. Note: A simple subject is never found in a prepositional phrase (a phrase beginning with a word such as of, by, over, through, until).

Present Tense Verb Form

	Singular	Plural
1st person (talking about oneself)	I do	We do
2nd person (talking to another)	You do	You do
3rd person (talking about someone or something)	He She does It	They do

Error: Sally, as well as her sister, plan to go into nursing.

Problem: The subject in the sentence is *Sally* alone, not the word *sister*. Therefore, the verb must be singular.

Correction: *Sally, as well as her sister, plans to go into nursing.*

Error: There has been many car accidents lately on that street.

Problem: The subject *accidents* in this sentence is plural; the verb must be plural also—even though it comes before the subject.

Correction: *There have been many car accidents lately on that street.*

Error: Everyone of us have a reason to attend the school musical.

Problem: The simple subject is *everyone*, not the *us* in the prepositional phrase. Therefore, the verb must be singular also.

Correction: *Everyone of us has a reason to attend the school musical.*

Error: Either the police captain or his officers is going to the convention.

Problem: In either/or and neither/nor constructions, the verb agrees with the subject closer to it.

Correction: *Either the police captain or his officers are going to the convention.*

PRACTICE EXERCISE—SUBJECT-VERB AGREEMENT

Choose the option that corrects an error in the underlined portion(s).
If no error exists, choose "No change is necessary."

1)   Every year, the store <u>stays</u> open late, when shoppers desperately <u>try</u> to purchase Christmas presents as they <u>prepare</u> for the holiday.

    A. stay
    B. tries
    C. prepared
    D. No change is necessary.

2)   Paul McCartney, together with George Harrison and Ringo Starr, <u>sing</u> classic Beatles songs on a special greatest-hits CD.

    A. singing
    B. sings
    C. sung
    D. No change is necessary.

3)   My friend's cocker spaniel, while <u>chasing</u> cats across the street, always <u>manages</u> to <u>knock</u> over the trash cans.

    A. chased
    B. manage
    C. knocks
    D. No change is necessary.

4)   Some of the ice on the driveway <u>have melted.</u>

    A. having melted
    B. has melted
    C. has melt.
    D. No change is necessary.

5) Neither the criminal forensics expert nor the DNA blood evidence <u>provide</u> enough support for that verdict.

    A. provides
    B. were providing
    C. are providing
    D. No change is necessary.

ANSWER KEY: PRACTICE EXERCISE FOR SUBJECT-VERB AGREEMENT

1) D   Option D is correct because *store* is third-person singular and requires the third-person singular verbs *stays*. Option B is incorrect because the plural noun *shoppers* requires a plural verb *try*. In Option C, there is no reason to shift to the past tense *prepared*.

2) B   Option B is correct because the subject, *Paul McCartney*, is singular and requires the singular verb *sings*. Option A is incorrect because the present participle *singing* does not stand alone as a verb. Option C is incorrect because the past participle *sung* alone cannot function as the verb in this sentence.

3) D   Option D is the correct answer because the subject *cocker spaniel* is singular and requires the singular verb *manages*. Options A, B, and C do not work structurally with the sentence.

4) B   The subject of the sentence is *some*, which requires a third-person singular verb *has melted*. Option A incorrectly uses the present participle *having*, which does not act as a helping verb. Option C does not work structurally with the sentence.

5) A   In Option A, the singular subject *evidence* is closer to the verb and thus requires the singular in the neither/nor construction. Both Options B and C are plural forms with the helping verb and the present participle.

Past tense and past participles

Both regular and irregular verbs must appear in their standard forms for each tense. Note: the -ed or -d ending is added to regular verbs in the past tense and for past participles.

Infinitive	Past Tense	Past Participle
Bake	Baked	Baked

Irregular Verb Forms

Infinitive	Past Tense	Past Participle
Be	Was, were	Been
Become	Became	Become
Break	Broke	Broken
Bring	Brought	Brought
Choose	Chose	Chosen
Come	Came	Come
Do	Did	Done
Draw	Drew	Drawn
Eat	Ate	Eaten
Fall	Fell	Fallen
Forget	Forgot	Forgotten
Freeze	Froze	Frozen
Give	Gave	Given
Go	Went	Gone
Grow	Grew	Grown
Have/has	Had	Had
Hide	Hid	Hidden
Know	Knew	Known
Lay	Laid	Laid
Lie	Lay	Lain
Ride	Rode	Ridden
Rise	Rose	Risen
Run	Ran	Run
See	Saw	Seen
Steal	Stole	Stolen
Take	Took	Taken
Tell	Told	Told
Throw	Threw	Thrown
Wear	Wore	Worn
Write	Wrote	Written

Error: She should have went to her doctor's appointment at the scheduled time.

Problem: The past participle of the verb *to go* is *gone*. *Went* expresses the simple past tense.

Correction: *She should have gone to her doctor's appointment at the scheduled time.*

Error: My train is suppose to arrive before two o'clock.

Problem: The verb following *train* is a present tense passive construction, which requires the present tense verb *to be* and the past participle.

Correction: *My train is supposed to arrive before two o'clock.*

Error: Linda should of known that the car wouldn't start after leaving it out in the cold all night.

Problem: *Should of* is a nonstandard expression. *Of* is not a verb.

Correction: *Linda should have known that the car wouldn't start after leaving it out in the cold all night.*

PRACTICE EXERCISE—STANDARD VERB FORMS

Choose the option that corrects an error in the underlined portion(s). If no error exists, choose "No change is necessary."

1) My professor <u>had knew</u> all along that we would pass his course.

    A. know
    B. had known
    C. knowing
    D. No change is necessary

2) Kevin was asked to erase the vulgar words he <u>had wrote.</u>

    A. writes
    B. has write
    C. had written
    D. No change is necessary

3) Melanie <u>had forget</u> to tell her parents that she left the cat in the closet.

    A. had forgotten
    B. forgot
    C. forget
    D. No change is necessary

4) Craig always <u>leave</u> the house a mess when his parents are not there.

    A. left
    B. leaves
    C. leaving
    D. No change is necessary

5) The store manager accused Kathy of <u>having stole</u> more than five hundred dollars from the safe.

    A. has stolen
    B. having stolen
    C. stole
    D. No change is necessary

ANSWER KEY: PRACTICE EXERCISE FOR STANDARD VERB FORMS

1. B   Option B is correct because the past participle needs the helping verb *had*. Option A is incorrect because *it* is in the infinitive tense. Option C incorrectly uses the present participle.

2. C   Option C is correct because the past participle follows the helping verb *had*. Option A uses the verb in the present tense. Option B is an incorrect use of the verb.

3. A   Option A is correct because the past participle uses the helping verb *had*. Option B uses the wrong form of the verb. Option C uses the wrong form of the verb.

4. B   Option B correctly uses the past tense of the verb. Option A uses the verb in an incorrect way. Option C uses the verb without a helping verb such as *is*.

5. B   Option B is correct because it is the past participle. Option A and C use the verb incorrectly.

Inappropriate shifts in verb tense

Verb tenses must refer to the same time consistently, unless a change in time is required.

Error: Despite the increased number of students in the school this year, overall attendance is higher last year at the sporting events.

Problem: The verb *is* represents an inconsistent shift to the present tense when the action refers to a past occurrence.

Correction: *Despite the increased number of students in the school this year, overall attendance was higher last year at sporting events.*

Error: My friend Lou, who just competed in the marathon, ran since he was twelve years old.

Problem: Because Lou continues to run, the present perfect tense is needed.

Correction: *My friend Lou, who just competed in the marathon, has run since he was twelve years old.*

Error: The Mayor congratulated Wallace Mangham, who renovates the city hall last year.

Problem: Although the speaker is talking in the present, the action of renovating the city hall was in the past.

Correction: *The Mayor congratulated Wallace Mangham, who renovated the city hall last year.*

PRACTICE EXERCISE—SHIFTS IN TENSE

Choose the option that corrects an error in the underlined portion(s). If no error exists, choose "No change is necessary."

1) After we <u>washed</u> the fruit that had <u>growing</u> in the garden, we knew there <u>was</u> a store that would buy them.

   A) washing
   B) grown
   C) is
   D) No change is necessary.

2) The tourists <u>used</u> to visit the Atlantic City boardwalk whenever they <u>vacationed</u> during the summer. Unfortunately, their numbers have <u>diminished</u> every year.

   A) use
   B) vacation
   C) diminish
   D) No change is necessary.

3) When the temperature <u>drops</u> to below thirty-two degrees Fahrenheit, the water on the lake <u>freezes</u>, which <u>allowed</u> children to skate across it.

   A) dropped
   B) froze
   C) allows
   D) No change is necessary.

4) The artists were <u>hired</u> to <u>create</u> a monument that would pay tribute to the men who were <u>killed</u> in World War II.

   A) hiring
   B) created
   C) killing
   D) No change is necessary.

5) Emergency medical personnel rushed to the scene of the shooting, where many injured people <u>waiting</u> for treatment.

   A) wait
   B) waited
   C) waits
   D) No change is necessary.

ANSWER KEY: PRACTICE EXERCISE FOR SHIFTS IN TENSE

1) B   The past participle *grown* is needed instead of *growing,* which is the progressive tense. Option A is incorrect because the past participle *washed* takes the *-ed*. Option C incorrectly replaces the past participle *was* with the present tense *is*.

2) D   Option A is incorrect because *use* is the present tense. Option B incorrectly uses the noun *vacation*. Option C incorrectly uses the present tense *diminish* instead of the past tense *diminished*.

3) C   The present tense *allows* is necessary in the context of the sentence. Option A is incorrect because *dropped* is a past participle. Option B is incorrect because *froze* is also a past participle.

4) D   Option A is incorrect because *hiring* is the present tense. Option B is incorrect because *created* is a past participle. In Option C, *killing* does not fit into the context of the sentence.

5) B   In Option B, *waited* corresponds with the past tense *rushed*. In Option A, *wait* is incorrect because it is present tense. In Option C, *waits* is incorrect because the noun *people* is plural and requires the singular form of the verb.

Skill 10.2   **Recognize the standard use of pronouns (e.g., pronoun-antecedent agreement; the use of possessive pronouns; the use of the relative pronouns who, whom, whose, which, and that; and the use of the demonstrative pronouns this, that, these, and those).**

Agreements between pronoun and antecedent

A pronoun must correspond to its antecedent in number (singular or plural), person (first, second, or third person) and gender (male, female, or neutral). A pronoun must refer clearly to a single word, not to a complete idea.

A **pronoun shift** is a grammatical error in which the author starts a sentence, paragraph, or section of a paper using one particular type of pronoun and then suddenly shifts to another. This often confuses the reader.

Error: A teacher should treat all their students fairly.

Problem: Since *teacher* is singular, the pronoun referring to it must also be singular. Otherwise, the noun has to be made plural.

Correction: *Teachers should treat all their students fairly.*

Error: When an actor is rehearsing for a play, it often helps if you can memorize the lines in advance.

Problem: *Actor* is a third-person word; that is, the writer is talking about the subject. The pronoun *you* is in the second person, which means the writer is talking to the subject.

Correction: *When actors are rehearsing for plays, it helps if they can memorize the lines in advance.*

Error: The workers in the factory were upset when his or her paychecks did not arrive on time.

Problem: *Workers* is a plural form, while *his or her* refers to one person.

Correction: *The workers in the factory were upset when their paychecks did not arrive on time.*

Error: The charity auction was highly successful, which pleased everyone.

Problem: In this sentence, the pronoun *which* refers to the idea of the auction's success. In fact, *which* has no antecedent in the sentence; the word *success* is not stated.

Correction: *Everyone was pleased at the success of the auction.*

Error: Lana told Melanie that she would like aerobics.

Problem: The person that she refers to is unclear; it could be either Lana or Melanie.

Correction: *Lana said that Melanie would like aerobics.*

-OR-

Lana told Melanie that she, Melanie, would like aerobics.

Error: I dislike accounting, even though my brother is one.

Problem: A person's occupation is not the same as a field, and the pronoun *one* is thus incorrect. Note that the word *accountant* is not used in the sentence, so *one* has no antecedent.

Correction: *I dislike accounting, even though my brother is an accountant.*

Error: In Todd's letter, he told his mom he'd broken the priceless vase.

Problem: In this sentence, the pronoun "he" seems to refer to the noun phrase "Todd's letter," though it was probably meant to refer to the possessive noun "Todd's."

Correction: In his letter, Todd told his mom that he had broken the priceless vase.

A pronoun should not refer to an implied idea.

A pronoun must refer to a specific antecedent rather than an implied antecedent. When an antecedent is not stated specifically, the reader has to guess or assume the meaning of a sentence. Pronouns that do not have antecedents are called expletives. "It" and "there" are the most common expletives, though other pronouns can also become expletives as well. In informal conversation, expletives allow for casual presentation of ideas without supporting evidence; however, in writing that is more formal, it is best to be more precise.

Error: She said that it is important to floss every day.

Problem: The pronoun "it" refers to an implied idea.

Correction: She said that flossing every day is important.

Error: They returned the book because there were missing pages.

Problem: The pronouns "they" and "there" do not refer to the antecedent.

Correction: The customer returned the book with missing pages.

Using Who, That, and Which

Who, whom and **whose** refer to human beings and can either introduce essential or nonessential clauses. **That** refers to things other than humans and it is used to introduce essential clauses. **Which** refers to things other than humans and it is used to introduce nonessential clauses.

Error: The doctor that performed the surgery said the man would be fully recovered.

Problem: Since the relative pronoun is referring to a human, who should be used.

Correction: The doctor who performed the surgery said the man would be fully recovered.

Error: That ice cream cone that you just ate looked delicious.

Problem: That has already been used so you must use *which* to introduce the next clause, whether it is essential or nonessential.

Correction: That ice cream cone, which you just ate, looked delicious.

Proper case forms

Pronouns, unlike nouns, change case forms. Pronouns must be in the subjective, objective, or possessive form according to their functions in the sentence.

Personal Pronouns

Subjective (Nominative)		Possessive		Objective	
	Singular	Plural	Singular	Plural	Singular	Plural
1st person	I	We	My	Our	Me	Us
2nd person	You	You	Your	Your	You	You
3rd person	He She It	They	His Her Its	Their	Him Her It	Them

Relative Pronouns
Who   Subjective/Nominative
Whom   Objective
Whose   Possessive

Error: Tom and me have reserved seats for next week's baseball game.

Problem: The pronoun *me* is the subject of the verb *have reserved* and should be in the subjective form.

Correction: *Tom and I have reserved seats for next week's baseball game.*

Error: Mr. Green showed all of we students how to make paper hats.

Problem: The pronoun *we* is the object of the preposition *of*. It should be in the objective form, *us*.

Correction: *Mr. Green showed all of us students how to make paper hats.*

Error: Who's coat is this?

Problem: The interrogative possessive pronoun is *whose*; *who's* is the contraction for who is.

Correction: *Whose coat is this?*

Error: The voters will choose the candidate whom has the best qualifications for the job.

Problem: The case of the relative pronoun *who* or *whom* is determined by the pronoun's function in the clause in which it appears. The word who is in the subjective case, and whom is in the objective. Analyze how the pronoun is being used within the sentence.

Correction: *The voters will choose the candidate who has the best qualifications for the job.*

PRACTICE EXERCISE—PRONOUN CASE

Choose the option that corrects an error in the underlined portion(s). If no error exists, choose "No change is necessary."

1)   Even though Sheila and <u>he</u> had planned to be alone at the diner, <u>they</u> were joined by three friends of <u>their's</u> instead.

    A) him
    B) him and her
    C) theirs
    D) No change is necessary.

2)   Uncle Walter promised to give his car to <u>whomever</u> will guarantee to drive it safely.

    A) whom
    B) whoever
    C) them
    D) No change is necessary.

3)   Eddie and <u>him</u> gently laid <u>the body</u> on the ground next to <u>the sign</u>.

        A) he
        B) them
        C) it
        D) No change is necessary.

4)   Mary, <u>who</u> is competing in the chess tournament, is a better player than <u>me</u>.

        A) whose
        B) whom
        C) I
        D) No change is necessary.

5)   <u>We, ourselves</u>, have decided not to buy property in that development; however, our friends have already bought <u>themselves</u> some land.

        A) We, ourself,
        B) their selves
        C) their self
        D) No change is necessary.

ANSWER KEY: PRACTICE EXERCISE FOR PRONOUN CASE

1) C   The possessive pronoun *theirs* does not need an apostrophe. Option A is incorrect because the subjective pronoun *he* is needed in this sentence. Option B is incorrect because the subjective pronoun *they*, not the objective pronouns *him* and *her*, is needed.

2) B   The subjective case *whoever*—not the objective case *whomever* —is the subject of the relative clause *whoever will guarantee to drive it safely*. Option A is incorrect because *whom* is an objective pronoun. Option C is incorrect because *car* is singular and takes the pronoun *it*.

3) A   The subjective pronoun *he* is needed as the subject of the verb *laid*. Option B is incorrect because *them* is vague; the noun *body* is needed to clarify *it*. Option C is incorrect because *it* is vague, and the noun *sign* is necessary for clarification.

4) C   The subjective pronoun *I* is needed because the comparison is understood. Option A incorrectly uses the possessive *whose*. Option B is incorrect because the subjective pronoun *who*, and not the objective *whom*, is needed.

5) D   The reflexive pronoun *themselves* refers to the plural *friends*. Option A is incorrect because the plural *we* requires the reflexive *ourselves*. Option C is incorrect because the possessive pronoun *their* is never joined with either *self* or *selves*.

Demonstrative pronouns

The four demonstrative pronouns are ***this, that, these,*** *and* ***those***.

This and *these* refer to something nearby in time and space.
That and *those* refer to something farther away in time and space.

This and *that* are singular.
These and *those* are plural.

These words can also be used as adjectives.

Examples:
This is an exciting book.
This is a singular pronoun and refers to the book, which is near the speaker.

This book is exciting.
This is a singular adjective and modifies *book,* which is near the speaker.

That is a classic-looking car.
That is a singular pronoun and refers to the car, which is away from the speaker.

That car is classic looking.
That is a singular adjective and modifies *car,* which is away from the speaker.

These are very interesting antiques.
These is a plural pronoun and refers to antiques, which are near the speaker.

These antiques are interesting.
These is a plural adjective and modifies the word *antiques*, which are near the speaker.

We bought those at the antique fair.
Those is a plural pronoun and refers to whatever was bought at the fair.

We bought those chairs at the antique fair.
Those is a plural adjective and modifies *chairs*, which are away from the speaker.

Skill 10.3   **Recognize the standard use of modifiers (e.g., adverbs, adjectives, comparatives, superlatives).**

Adjectives are words that modify or describe nouns or pronouns. Adjectives usually precede the words they modify, but not always; for example, an adjective occurs after a linking verb.

Adverbs are words that modify verbs, adjectives, or other adverbs. They cannot modify nouns. Adverbs answer such questions as how, why, when, where, how much, or how often something is done. Many adverbs are formed by adding -ly.

Error: The birthday cake tasted sweetly.

Problem: *Tasted* is a linking verb; the modifier that follows should be an adjective, not an adverb.

Correction: *The birthday cake tasted sweet.*

Error: You have done good with this project.

Problem: *Good* is an adjective and cannot be used to modify a verb phrase such as *have done.*

Correction: *You have done well with this project.*

Error: The coach was positive happy about the team's chance of winning.

Problem: The adjective *positive* cannot be used to modify another adjective, *happy.* An adverb is needed instead.

Correction: *The coach was positively happy about the team's chance of winning.*

Error: The fireman acted quick and brave to save the child from the burning building.

Problem: *Quick and brave* are adjectives and cannot be used to describe a verb. Adverbs are needed instead.

Correction: *The fireman acted quickly and bravely to save the child from the burning building.*

PRACTICE EXERCISE—ADJECTIVES AND ADVERBS

Choose the option that corrects an error in the underlined portion(s).
If no error exists, choose "No change is necessary."

1) Moving <u>quick</u> throughout the house, the burglar <u>removed</u> several priceless antiques before <u>carelessly</u> dropping his wallet.

   A) quickly
   B) remove
   C) careless
   D) No change is necessary.

2) The car <u>crashed loudly</u> into the retaining wall before spinning <u>wildly</u> on the sidewalk.

   A) crashes
   B) loudly
   C) wild
   D) No change is necessary.

3) The airplane <u>landed safe</u> on the runway after <u>nearly</u> colliding with a helicopter.

   A) land
   B) safely
   C) near
   D) No change is necessary.

4) The <u>horribly bad</u> special effects in the movie disappointed us <u>great</u>.

   A) horrible
   B) badly
   C) greatly
   D) No change is necessary.

5) The man promised to obey the rules of the social club <u>faithfully</u>.

   A) faithful
   B) faithfulness
   C) faith
   D) No change is necessary.

ANSWER KEY: PRACTICE EXERCISE FOR ADJECTIVES AND ADVERBS

1) A The adverb *quickly* is needed to modify *moving*. Option B is incorrect because it uses the wrong form of the verb. Option C is incorrect because the adverb *carelessly* is needed before the verb *dropping,* not the adjective *careless*.

2) D The sentence is correct as it is written. Adverbs *loudly* and *wildly* are needed to modify *crashed* and *spinning*. Option A incorrectly uses the verb *crashes* instead of the participle *crashing*, which acts as an adjective.

3) B The adverb *safely* is needed to modify the verb *landed*. Option A is incorrect because *land* is a noun. Option C is incorrect because *near* is an adjective, not an adverb.

4) C The adverb *greatly* is needed to modify the verb *disappointed*. Option A is incorrect because *horrible* is an adjective, not an adverb. Option B is incorrect because *bad* needs to modify the adverb *horribly*.

5) D The adverb *faithfully* is the correct modifier of the verb *promised*. Option A is an adjective used to modify nouns. Neither Option B nor Option C, which are both nouns, is a modifier.

Appropriate comparative and superlative degree forms

When comparisons are made, the correct form of the adjective or adverb must be used. The comparative form is used for two items. The superlative form is used for more than two.

	Comparative	Superlative
slow	slower	slowest
young	younger	youngest
tall	taller	tallest

With some words, more and most are used to make comparisons instead of -er and -est.

quiet	more quiet	most quiet
energetic	more energetic	most energetic
quick	more quickly	most quickly

Comparisons must be made between similar structures or items. In the sentence, "My house is similar in color to Steve's," one house is being compared to another house, as understood by the use of the possessive Steve's.

On the other hand, if the sentence reads, "My house is similar in color to Steve," the comparison would be faulty because it would be comparing the house to Steve, not to Steve's house.

Error: Last year's rides at the carnival were bigger than this year.

Problem: In the sentence as it is worded above, the rides at the carnival are being compared to this year, not to this year's rides.

Correction: *Last year's rides at the carnival were bigger than this year's.*

PRACTICE EXERCISE—LOGICAL COMPARISONS

Choose the sentence that logically and correctly expresses the comparison.

1)   A. This year's standards are higher than last year.
      B. This year's standards are more high than last year.
      C. This year's standards are higher than last year's.

2)   A. Tom's attitudes are very different from his father's.
      B. Toms attitudes are very different from his father.
      C. Tom's attitudes are very different from his father.

3)   A. John is the stronger member of the gymnastics team.
      B. John is the strongest member of the gymnastics team.
      C. John is the most strong member of the gymnastics team.

4)   A. Tracy's book report was longer than Tony's.
      B. Tracy's book report was more long than Tony's.
      C. Tracy's book report was longer than Tony.

5)   A. Becoming a lawyer is as difficult as, if not more difficult than, becoming a doctor.

      B. Becoming a lawyer is as difficult, if not more difficult than, becoming a doctor.

      C. Becoming a lawyer is difficult, if not more difficult than, becoming a doctor.

6)   A. Better than any movie of the modern era, *Schindler's List* portrays the destructiveness of hate.

      B. More better than any movie of the modern era, *Schindler's List* portrays the destructiveness of hate.

      C. Better than any other movie of the modern era, *Schindler's List* portrays the destructiveness of hate.

ANSWER KEY: PRACTICE EXERCISE FOR LOGICAL COMPARISONS

1) C   Option C is correct because the comparison is between this year's standards and last year's [standards is understood]. Option A compares the standards to last year. In Option B, the faulty comparative *more high* should be *higher*.

2) A   Option A is incorrect because Tom's attitudes are compared to his father's [attitudes is understood]. Option B deletes the necessary apostrophe to show possession (Tom's), and the comparison is faulty with *attitudes* compared to father. While Option C uses the correct possessive, it retains the faulty comparison shown in Option B.

3) B   In Option B, John is correctly the strongest member of a team that consists of more than two people. Option A uses the comparative *stronger* (comparison of two items) rather than the superlative *strongest* (comparison of more than two). Option C uses a faulty superlative, *most strong*.

4) A   Option A is correct because the comparison is between Tracy's book report and Tony's (book report). Option B uses the faulty comparative *more long* instead of longer. Option C wrongly compares Tracy's book report to Tony.

5) A   In Option A, the dual comparison is correctly stated: *as difficult as, if not more difficult than*. Remember to test the dual comparison by taking out the intervening comparison. Option B deletes the necessary *as* after the first *difficult*. Option C deletes the *as* before and after the first *difficult*.

6) C   Option C includes the necessary word *other* in the comparison *better than any other movie*. The comparison in Option A is not complete, and Option B uses a faulty comparative *more better*.

Skill 10.3 **Recognize the correct use of commonly misused words (e.g., their/there/they're, to/too).**

Students frequently encounter problems with homonyms—words that are spelled and pronounced the same as another but that have different meanings such as *mean*, a verb, "to intend"; *mean* an adjective, "unkind"; and *mean* a noun or adjective, "average." These words are actually both homonyms and homographs (written the same way).

A similar phenomenon that causes trouble is heteronyms (also sometimes called heterophones), words that are spelled the same but have different pronunciations and meanings (in other words, they are homographs that differ in pronunciation or, technically, homographs that are not homophones). For example, the homographs *desert* (abandon) and *desert* (arid region) are heteronyms (pronounced differently); but *mean* (intend) and *mean* (average) are not. They are pronounced the same, or are homonyms.

Another similar occurrence in English is the capitonym, a word that is spelled the same but has different meanings when it is capitalized and may or may not have different pronunciations. Example: *polish* (to make shiny) and *Polish* (from Poland).

Some of the most troubling homonyms are those that are spelled differently but sound the same.

It's and Its
   it's: the contraction for "it is"

   Its: 3rd person singular neuter pronoun that shows possession

   Example: It's amazing to watch the turtle retreat into **its** shell.

There/Their/They're
   there: adverb showing location

   their: 3rd person plural pronoun that show possession

   they're: contraction for they are

   Example: They're very careful about placing **their** products on the floor over **there**.

To, Too, Two
> *To:* preposition
> *Too:* adverb meaning also or showing intensity
> *Two:* number

> **Example**: She bought **too** many items when she went **to** the store **two** times last week.

Some homonyms/homographs are particularly complicated and troubling. Fluke, for instance is a fish, a flatworm, the end parts of an anchor, the fins on a whale's tail, and a stroke of luck.

Common Troublesome Words to Student Writers:

accept: tolerate; *except*: everything but.

add: put together with; *ad*: short for advertisement.

allowed: permitted; *aloud*: audibly.

allot: to distribute, allocate; *a lot* (often "*alot*"): much, many (a lot of).

allusion: indirect reference; *illusion*: a distortion of sensory perception.

bare: naked, exposed or very little (bare necessities); *bear*: as a noun, a large mammal and as a verb, to carry.

boy: a male adolescent or child; *buoy*: a floating marker in the sea.

bridal: pertaining to a bride (bridal gown, bridal suite); *bridle*: part of a horse's tack.

capital: punishable by death; with an upper-case letter, principal town or city, or wealth and money; *Capitol*: the home of the Congress of the United States and some other legislatures.

chord: group of musical notes; *cord*: rope, long electrical line.

compliment: a praising or flattering remark; *complement*: something that completes.

discreet: tactful or diplomatic; *discrete*: separate or distinct.

dyeing: artificially coloring; *dying*: passing away.

effect: outcome; *affect*: have an effect on.

gorilla: the largest of the great apes; *guerrilla*: a small combat group.

hair: an outgrowth of the epidermis in mammals; *hare*: rabbit.

hoard: to accumulate and store up; *horde*: large group of warriors, mob.

lam: U.S. slang "on the lam" means "on the run"; *lamb*: a young sheep.

lead: pronounced to rhyme with "seed," to guide or serve as the head of; *lead*: pronounced to rhyme with "head," a heavy metal; *led*: the past tense of "lead."

medal: an award to be strung around the neck; *meddle*: stick one's nose into others' affairs; *metal*: shiny, malleable element or alloy like silver or gold; *mettle*: toughness, guts.

morning: the time between midnight and midday; *mourning*: period of grieving after a death.

past: time before now (past, present and future); *passed*: past tense of "to pass."

piece: portion; *peace*: opposite of war.

peak: tip, height, to reach its highest point; *peek*: to take a brief look; *pique*: fit of anger; to incite (pique one's interest).

Here are a few strategies to help students conquer these demons:

- Practice using them in sentences.
- Determine context to help understand the difference.
- Drill if necessary to overcome the misuses.

COMPETENCY 11.0   APPLY KNOWLEDGE OF MECHANICAL CONVENTIONS IN STANDARD ENGLISH.

Skill 11.1   Identify and correct examples in which incorrect or extraneous punctuation has been used (e.g., commas, periods, exclamation points, apostrophes, quotation marks, semicolons joining clauses, colons to begin a list) or necessary punctuation has been omitted.

Commas

Commas indicate a brief pause. They are used to set off dependent clauses and long introductory word groups, to separate words in a series, to set off unimportant material that interrupts the flow of the sentence, and to separate independent clauses joined by conjunctions.

Error: After I finish my master's thesis I plan to work in Chicago.

Problem: A comma is needed after an introductory dependent word group containing a subject and verb.

Correction: *After I finish my master's thesis, I plan to work in Chicago.*

Error: I washed waxed and vacuumed my car today.

Problem: Commas should separate nouns, phrases, or clauses in a list, as well as two or more coordinate adjectives that modify one word. Although the word *and* is sometimes considered optional, it is often necessary to clarify the meaning.

Correction: *I washed, waxed, and vacuumed my car today.*

Error: She was a talented dancer but she is mostly remembered for her singing ability.

Problem: A comma is needed before a conjunction that joins two independent clauses (complete sentences).

Correction: *She was a talented dancer, but she is mostly remembered for her singing ability.*

Periods

Periods are used as end marks to declarative and imperative sentences. A declarative sentence makes a statement. An imperative sentence makes a request or issues a command.

- Declarative sentence: Now is the winter of our discontent.

- Imperative sentence: Please sign your name to this contract.

Periods are used in other cases as well:

- An indirect question: She wondered when the train would come.

- In abbreviations: Dr. White arrived in Washington, D.C., at 10: a.m.

- As decimal points: With tax, my lunch was $10.85.

Exclamation Points
Use exclamation points to express strong feeling, emotion, or urgency.

- Wow, what a day!
- I hate spinach!
- Hurry or we'll miss the bus!

To show especially strong feeling, writers may want to use more than one exclamation point. Generally, three are sufficient!!! But this type of strong expression is not used in formal writing.

Semicolons and colons

Semicolons are needed to separate two or more closely related independent clauses when the second clause is introduced by a transitional adverb. (These clauses may also be written as separate sentences, preferably by placing the adverb within the second sentence). **Colons** are used to introduce lists and to emphasize what follows.

Error: I climbed to the top of the mountain, it took me three hours.

Problem: A comma alone cannot separate two independent clauses. Instead, a semicolon is needed to separate two related sentences.

Correction: *I climbed to the top of the mountain; it took me three hours.*

Error: In the movie, asteroids destroyed Dallas, Texas, Kansas City, Missouri, and Boston, Massachusetts.

Problem: Semicolons are needed to separate items in a series that already contain internal punctuation.

Correction: *In the movie, asteroids destroyed Dallas, Texas; Kansas City, Missouri; and Boston, Massachusetts.*

Error: Essays will receive the following grades, A for excellent, B for good, C for average, and D for unsatisfactory.

Problem: A colon is needed to emphasize the information or list that follows.

Correction: *Essays will receive the following grades: A for excellent, B for good, C for average, and D for unsatisfactory.*

Error: The school carnival included: amusement rides, clowns, food booths, and a variety of games.

Problem: The material preceding the colon and the list that follows is not a complete sentence. Do not separate a verb (or preposition) from the object.

Correction: *The school carnival included amusement rides, clowns, food booths, and a variety of games.*

Apostrophes

Apostrophes are used to show either contractions or possession.

Error: She shouldnt be permitted to smoke cigarettes in the building.

Problem: An apostrophe is needed in a contraction in place of the missing letter.

Correction: *She shouldn't be permitted to smoke cigarettes in the building.*

Error: My cousins motorcycle was stolen from his driveway.

Problem: An apostrophe is needed to show possession.

Correction: *My cousin's motorcycle was stolen from his driveway.*
(Note: The use of the apostrophe before the letter "s" means that there is just one cousin. The plural form would read the following way: My cousins' motorcycle was stolen from their driveway.)

Error: The childrens new kindergarten teacher was also a singer.

Problem: An apostrophe is needed to show possession.

Correction: *The children's' new kindergarten teacher was also a singer.*

Error: Children screams could be heard for miles.

Problem: An apostrophe and the letter *s* are needed in the sentence to show whose screams they are.

Correction: *Children's screams could be heard for miles.*
(Note: Because the word children is already plural, the apostrophe and *s* must be added afterward to show ownership.)

Quotation marks

In a quoted statement that is either declarative or imperative, place the period inside the closing quotation marks.

"The airplane crashed on the runway during takeoff."

If the quotation is followed by other words in the sentence, place a comma inside the closing quotations marks and a period at the end of the sentence.

"The airplane crashed on the runway during takeoff," said the announcer.

In most instances in which a quoted title or expression occurs at the end of a sentence, the period is placed before either the single or double quotation marks.

"The middle school readers were unprepared to understand Bryant's poem 'Thanatopsis.'"

Early book-length adventure stories such as *Don Quixote* and *The Three Musketeers* were known as "picaresque novels."

The final quotation mark would precede the period if the content of the sentence were about a speech or quote so that the understanding of the meaning would be confused by the placement of the period.

The first thing out of his mouth was, "Hi, I'm home."
-but-
The first line of his speech began, "I arrived home to an empty house".

In sentences that are interrogatory or exclamatory, the question mark or exclamation point should be positioned outside the closing quotation marks if the quote itself is a statement or command or cited title.

Who decided to lead us in the recitation of the "Pledge of Allegiance"?

Why was Tillie shaking as she began her recitation, "Once upon a midnight dreary..."?

I was embarrassed when Mrs. White said, "Your slip is showing"!

In sentences that are declarative, but the quotation is a question or an exclamation, place the question mark or exclamation point inside the quotation marks.

> The hall monitor yelled, "Fire! Fire!"

> "Fire! Fire!" yelled the hall monitor.

> Cory shrieked, "Is there a mouse in the room?" (In this instance, the question supersedes the exclamation.)

Quotations—whether words, phrases, or clauses—should be punctuated according to the rules of the grammatical function they serve in the sentence.

> The works of Shakespeare, "the bard of Avon," have been contested as originating with other authors.

> "You'll get my money," the old man warned, "when 'Hell freezes over'."

> Sheila cited the passage that began "Four score and seven years ago...." (Note the ellipsis followed by an enclosed period.)

> "Old Ironsides" inspired the preservation of the U. S. S. Constitution.

Use quotation marks to enclose the titles of shorter works: songs, short poems, short stories, essays, and chapters of books. (See "Using Italics" for punctuating longer titles.)

> "The Tell-Tale Heart"   "Casey at the Bat"   "America the Beautiful"

Dashes and Italics

Place **dashes** to denote sudden breaks in thought.

> Some periods in literature—the Romantic Age, for example— spanned different periods in different countries.

Use dashes instead of commas if commas are already used elsewhere in the sentence for amplification or explanation.

> The Fireside Poets included three Brahmans—James Russell Lowell, Henry David Wadsworth, Oliver Wendell Holmes— and John Greenleaf Whittier.

Use **italics** to punctuate the titles of long works of literature, names of periodical publications, musical scores, works of art and motion picture television, and radio programs. (When unable to write in italics, students should be instructed to underline in their own writing where italics would be appropriate.)

The Idylls of the King	*Hiawatha*	*The Sound and the Fury*
Mary Poppins	*Newsweek*	*The Nutcracker Suite*

Skill 11.2 Apply standards for capitalization.

Capitalize all proper names of persons (including specific organizations or agencies of government); places (countries, states, cities, parks, and specific geographical areas); and things (political parties, structures, historical and cultural terms, and calendar and time designations); and religious terms (any deity, revered person or group, sacred writings).

Percy Bysshe Shelley, Argentina, Mount Rainier National Park, Grand Canyon, League of Nations, the Sears Tower, Birmingham, Lyric Theater, Americans, Midwesterners, Democrats, Renaissance, Boy Scouts of America, Easter, God, Bible, Dead Sea Scrolls, Koran

Capitalize proper adjectives and titles used with proper names.

California Gold Rush, President John Adams, French fries, Homeric epic, Romanesque architecture, Senator John Glenn

Note: Some words that represent titles and offices are not capitalized unless used with a proper name.

Capitalized	Not Capitalized
Congressman McKay	the congressman from Florida
Commander Alger	commander of the Pacific Fleet
Queen Elizabeth	the queen of England

Capitalize all main words in titles of works of literature, art, and music.

Error: Emma went to Dr. Peters for treatment since her own Doctor was on vacation.

Problem: The use of capital letters with Emma and Dr .Peters is correct since they are specific (proper) names; the title Dr. is also capitalized. However, the word *doctor* is not a specific name and should not be capitalized.

Correction: *Emma went to Dr. Peters for treatment since her own doctor was on vacation.*

Error: Our Winter Break does not start until next wednesday.

Problem: Days of the week are capitalized, but seasons are not capitalized.

Correction: *Our winter break does not start until next Wednesday.*

Error: The exchange student from israel, who came to study Biochemistry, spoke spanish very well.

Problem: Languages and the names of countries are always capitalized. Courses are also capitalized when they refer to a specific course; they are not capitalized when they refer to courses in general.

Correction: *The exchange student from Israel, who came to study Biochemistry, spoke Spanish very well.*

Skill 11.3   Identify misspelled words in a sentence or passage.

Plural nouns

A good dictionary should replace the multiplicity and complexity of spelling rules based on phonics, letter doubling, and exceptions to rules not mastered by adulthood. As spelling mastery is also difficult for adolescents, our recommendation is the same. Learning the use of a dictionary and thesaurus will be a more rewarding use of time.

Most plurals of nouns that end in hard consonants or hard consonant sounds followed by a silent *e* are made by adding -*s*. Some words ending in vowels only add -*s*.

   fingers, numerals, banks, bugs, riots, homes, gates, radios, bananas

Nouns that end in soft consonant sounds *s, j, x, z, ch,* and *sh,* add -*es.* Some nouns ending in *o* add -es.

> dresses, waxes, churches, brushes, tomatoes

Nouns ending in *y* preceded by a vowel just add -*s.*

> boys, alleys

Nouns ending in *y* preceded by a consonant change the *y* to *i* and add -*es.*

> babies, corollaries, frugalities, poppies

Some nouns' plurals are formed irregularly or remain the same.

> sheep, deer, children, leaves, oxen

Some nouns derived from foreign words, especially Latin, may make their plurals in two different ways—one of them Anglicized. Sometimes, the meanings are the same; other times, the two plurals are used in slightly different contexts. It is always wise to consult the dictionary.

> appendices, appendixes   criterion, criteria
> indexes, indices   crisis, crises

Make the plurals of closed (solid) compound words in the usual way except for words ending in –*ful,* which make their plurals on the root word.

> timelines, hairpins

Make the plurals of open or hyphenated compounds by adding the change in inflection to the word that changes in number.

> fathers-in-law, courts-martial, masters of art, doctors of medicine

Make the plurals of letters, numbers, and abbreviations by adding -*s.*

> fives and tens, IBMs, 1990s, *p*s and *q*s (Note that letters are italicized.)

Possessive nouns

Make the possessives of singular nouns by adding an apostrophe followed by the letter *s* (*s).*

> baby's bottle, father's job, elephant's eye, teacher's desk, sympathizer's protests, week's postponement

Make the possessive of singular nouns ending in *s* by adding either an apostrophe or an (*'s*) depending upon common usage or sound. When making the possessive causes difficulty, use a prepositional phrase instead. Even with the sibilant ending, with a few exceptions, it is advisable to use the (*'s*) construction.

> dress's color, species' characteristics or characteristics of the species, James' hat or James's hat, Delores's shirt.

Make the possessive of plural nouns ending in *s* by adding the apostrophe after the *s*.

> horses' coats, jockeys' times, four days' time

Make possessives of plural nouns that do not end in *s* the same as singular nouns by adding *'s*.

> children's shoes, deer's antlers, cattle's horns

Make possessives of compound nouns by adding the inflection at the end of the word or phrase.

> the mayor of Los Angeles' campaign, the mailman's new truck, the mailmen's new trucks, my father-in-law's first wife, the keepsakes' values, several daughters-in-law's husbands

Note: Because a gerund functions as a noun, any noun preceding it and operating as a possessive adjective must reflect the necessary inflection. However, if the gerundive following the noun is a participle, no inflection is added.

> The general was perturbed by the private's sleeping on duty. (The word *sleeping* is a gerund, the object of the preposition *by*.
> *-but-*
> The general was perturbed to see the private sleeping on duty. (The word *sleeping* is a participle modifying *private*.)

COMPETENCY 12.0   IMPROVE INEFFECTIVE WRITING BY ANALYZING AND REVISING SENTENCES CONTAINING PROBLEMS RELATED TO GRAMMAR AND USAGE, CONSTRUCTION, AND MECHANICS.

Skill 12.1   Revise sentences to correct problems relating to grammar and usage (e.g., syntax, pronoun-antecedent agreement, subject-verb agreement, misplaced modifiers).

See also 10.1

In learning to write and in improving one's writing, the most useful exercise is editing/revising. Extensive revision is the hallmark of most successful writers. In the past, writers, student writers in particular, have been reluctant to revise because it meant beginning over to prepare the document for final presentation. However, that time is long gone. The writing of graduate dissertations took on a whole new dimension after the creation of the word processor and before long, classroom writing teachers were able to use this function to help students improve their writing.

Requiring extensive revision in writing classrooms nowadays is not unreasonable and can be an important stage in production of papers. Microsoft Word has had a "tracking" capability in its last several upgrades, which carries revision a step further. Now the teacher and student can carry on a dialogue on the paper itself. The teacher's deletions and additions can be tracked, the student can respond, and the tracking will be facilitated by automatically putting the changes in a different color. The "comment" function makes it possible for both teacher and student to write notes at the exactly relevant point in the manuscript.

While a spelling checker is an appropriate first step, students should be reminded that they should not rely solely on spell checkers for proofreading. Noted for their failure to understand context, spell checkers will not help with incorrect homonyms or typos.

Proofreading

Students proofread the draft for punctuation and mechanical errors. There are a few key points to remember when helping students learn to edit and proofread their work.

- It is crucial that students are not taught grammar in isolation but in the context of the writing process
- Ask students to read their writing and check for specific errors, like using a subordinate clause as a sentence
- Provide students with a proofreading checklist to guide them as they edit their work

Proofreading is checking mechanics, grammar, and spelling and should not be confused with editing. While software programs can help with these mechanics, they are not perfect. The writer is the final arbiter.

In addition to the information found in Sections 11.1, 11.2, and 11.3, here are some additional ways to improve sentence structure.

Misplaced and Dangling Modifiers

Particular phrases that are not placed near the one word they modify often result in misplaced modifiers. Particular phrases that do not relate to the subject being modified result in dangling modifiers.

Error: Weighing the options carefully, a decision was made regarding the punishment of the convicted murderer.

Problem: Who is weighing the options? No one capable of weighing is named in the sentence; thus, the participle phrase *weighing the options carefully* dangles. This problem can be corrected by adding a subject of the sentence capable of doing the action.

Correction: *Weighing the options carefully, the judge made a decision regarding the punishment of the convicted murderer.*

Error: Returning to my favorite watering hole, brought back many fond memories.

Problem: The person who returned is never indicated, and the participle phrase dangles. This problem can be corrected by creating a dependent clause from the modifying phrase.

Correction: *When I returned to my favorite watering hole, many fond memories came back to me.*

Error: One damaged house stood only to remind townspeople of the hurricane.

Problem: The placement of the misplaced modifier only suggests that the sole reason the house remained was to serve as a reminder. The faulty modifier creates ambiguity.

Correction: *Only one damaged house stood, reminding townspeople of the hurricane.*

PRACTICE EXERCISE—MISPLACED AND DANGLING MODIFIERS

Choose the sentence that expresses the thought most clearly and effectively and that has no error in structure.

1)   A. Attempting to remove the dog from the well, the paramedic tripped and fell in also.

   B. As the paramedic attempted to remove the dog from the well, he tripped and fell in also.

   C. The paramedic tripped and fell in also attempting to remove the dog from the well.

2)   A. To save the wounded child, a powerful explosion ripped through the operating room as the doctors worked.

   B. In the operating room, as the wounded child was being saved, a powerful explosion ripped through.

   C. To save the wounded child, the doctors worked as an explosion ripped through the operating room.

3)   A. One hot July morning, a herd of giraffes screamed wildly in the jungle next to the wildlife habitat.

   B. One hot July morning, a herd of giraffes screamed in the jungle wildly next to the wildlife habitat.

   C. One hot July morning, a herd of giraffes screamed in the jungle next to the wildlife habitat, wildly.

4)   A. Looking through the file cabinets in the office, the photographs of the crime scene revealed a new suspect in the investigation.

   B. Looking through the file cabinets in the office, the detective discovered photographs of the crime scene which revealed a new suspect in the investigation.

   C. A new suspect in the investigation was revealed in photographs of the crime scene that were discovered while looking through the file cabinets in the office.

ANSWER KEY: PRACTICE EXERCISE FOR MISPLACED AND DANGLING MODIFIERS

1) B   Option B corrects the dangling participle *attempting to remove the dog from the well* by creating a dependent clause introducing the main clause. In Option A, the introductory participle phrase *Attempting...well* does not refer to a paramedic, the subject of the main clause. The word *also* in Option C incorrectly implies that the paramedic was doing something besides trying to remove the dog.

2) C   Option C corrects the dangling modifier *to save the wounded child* by adding the concrete subject doctors worked. Option A infers that an explosion was working to save the wounded child. Option B never tells who was trying to save the wounded child.

3) A   Option A places the adverb *wildly* closest to the verb *screamed*, which it modifies. Both Options B and C incorrectly place the modifier away from the verb.

4) B   Option B corrects the modifier *looking through the file cabinets in the office* by placing it next to the detective who is doing the looking. Option A sounds as though the photographs were looking; Option C has no one doing the looking.

Faulty Parallelism

Two or more elements stated in a single clause should be expressed with the same (or parallel) structure (e.g., all adjectives, all verb forms, or all nouns).

Error: She needed to be beautiful, successful, and have fame.

Problem: The phrase *to be* is followed by two different structures: *beautiful* and *successful* are adjectives and *have fame* is a verb phrase.

Correction: *She needed to be <u>beautiful</u>, <u>successful</u>, and <u>famous</u>.*
                  (adjective) (adjective)   (adjective)

-OR-

She needed <u>beauty</u>, <u>success</u>, and <u>fame</u>.
           (noun)   (noun)   (noun)

Error: I plan either to sell my car during the spring or during the summer.

Problem: Paired conjunctions (also called correlative conjunctions—such as either-or, both-and, neither-nor, not only-but also) need to be followed with similar structures. In the sentence above, *either* is followed by *to sell my car during the spring*, while *or* is followed only by the phrase *during the summer*.

Correction: *I plan to sell my car during either the spring or the summer.*

Error: The President pledged to lower taxes and that he would cut spending to lower the national debt.

Problem: Since the phrase *to lower taxes* follows the verb *pledged*, a similar structure of *to* is needed with the phrase *cut spending*.

Correction: *The President pledged to lower taxes and to cut spending to lower the national debt.*

-OR-

The President pledged that he would lower taxes and cut spending to lower the national debt.

PRACTICE EXERCISE—PARALLELISM

Choose the sentence that expresses the thought most clearly and effectively and that has no error in structure.

1. A. Andy found the family tree, researches the Irish descendents, and he was compiling a book for everyone to read.

    B. Andy found the family tree, researched the Irish descendents, and compiled a book for everyone to read.

    C. Andy finds the family tree, researched the Irish descendents, and compiled a book for everyone to read.

2. A. In the last ten years, computer technology has advanced so quickly that workers have had difficulty keeping up with the new equipment and the increased amount of functions.

    B. Computer technology has advanced so quickly in the last ten years that workers have had difficulty to keep up with the new equipment and by increasing amount of functions.

    C. In the last ten years, computer technology has advanced so quickly that workers have had difficulty keeping up with the new equipment and the amount of functions are increasing.

3. A. The Florida State History Museum contains exhibits honoring famous residents, a video presentation about the state's history, an art gallery featuring paintings and sculptures, and they even display a replica of the Florida Statehouse.

    B. The Florida State History Museum contains exhibits honoring famous residents, a video presentation about the state's history, an art gallery featuring paintings and sculptures, and even a replica of the Florida Statehouse.

    C. The Florida State History Museum contains exhibits honoring famous residents, a video presentation about the state's history, an art gallery featuring paintings and sculptures, and there is even a replica of the Florida Statehouse.

4. A. Either the criminal justice students had too much practical experience and limited academic preparation or too much academic preparation and little practical experience.

    B. The criminal justice students either had too much practical experience and limited academic preparation or too much academic preparation and little practical experience.

    C. The criminal justice students either had too much practical experience and limited academic preparation or had too much academic preparation and little practical experience.

5. A. Filmmaking is an arduous process in which the producer hires the cast and crew, chooses locations for filming, supervises the actual production, and guides the editing.

    B. Because it is an arduous process, filmmaking requires the producer to hire a cast and crew and choose locations, supervise the actual production, and guides the editing.

    C. Filmmaking is an arduous process in which the producer hires the cast and crew, chooses locations for filming, supervises the actual production, and guided the editing.

ANSWER KEY: PRACTICE EXERCISE FOR PARALLELISM

1. B   Option B uses parallelism by presenting a series of past tense verbs: *found, researched*, and *compiled*. Option A interrupts the parallel structure of past tense verbs: *found, researches*, and *he was compiling*. Option C uses present tense verbs and then shifts to past tense: *finds, researched*, and *compiled*.

2. A   Option A uses parallel structure at the end of the sentence: *the new equipment and the increased amount of functions*. Option B creates a faulty structure with *to keep up with the new equipment and by increasing amount of functions*. Option C creates faulty parallelism with *the amount of functions are increasing*.

3. B   Option B uses parallelism by presenting a series of noun phrases acting as objects of the verb *contains*. Option A interrupts that parallelism by inserting *they even display*, and Option C interrupts the parallelism with the addition of *there is*.

4. C   In the either-or parallel construction, look for a balance on both sides. Option C creates that balanced parallel structure—*either had...or had*. Options A and B do not create the balance. In Option A, the structure is *Either the students...or too much*. In Option B, the structure is *either had...or too much*.

5. A   Option A uses parallelism by presenting a series of verbs with objects—*hires the cast and crew, chooses locations for filming, supervises the actual production, and guides the editing*. The structure of Option B incorrectly suggests that filmmaking chooses locations, supervises the actual production, and guides the editing. Option C interrupts the series of present tense verbs by inserting the participle *guided*, instead of the present tense *guides*.

Use of negatives in sentence formation:

Positive	Negative

To Be

Positive	Negative
I am afraid of the dark.	I am not afraid of the dark. (I'm not)
You are going to the store.	You are not going to the store (you're not / aren't)
They were pretty flowers.	They were not pretty flowers. (weren't)
I was enjoying my day off.	I was not enjoying my day off (wasn't)

Conditionals

Positive	Negative
Charlotte will arrive at 8.	Charlotte will not arrive at 8. (won't arrive)
Robert can run 26 miles.	Robert cannot run 26 miles (can't run)
I could have been great!	I could not have been great. (couldn't have)

Present simple

Positive	Negative
I want to go home.	I do not want to go home (don't)
Veronica walks too slowly.	Veronica does not walk too slowly. (doesn't)

Past Simple

Positive	Negative
I skipped rope daily.	I did not skip rope daily. (didn't)

Present Perfect

Positive	Negative
My mom has made my costume.	My mom has not made my costume. (hasn't)
The Thompsons have just bought a dog.	The Thompsons have not just bought a dog. (haven't)

Have Versus Have Got

Positive	Negative
I have 2 sisters.	I do not have two sisters.
I have got 2 sisters.	I have not got two sisters.
Jeremy has school tomorrow.	Jeremy does not have school tomorrow.
Jeremy has got school tomorrow.	Jeremy hasn't got school tomorrow.

Common negative words include:
no, not, none, nothing, nowhere, neither, nobody, no one, hardly, scarcely, barely.

A **double negative** occurs when two forms of negation are used in the same sentence. In order to correct a double negative, one of the negative words should be removed.

Error: I haven't got nothing.

Correction: I haven't got anything.

                   -OR-

                   I have nothing.

Error: Don't nobody leave until 7 o'clock.

Correction: Do not leave until 7 o'clock.

                   -OR-

                   Nobody leave until 7 o'clock.

It is also incorrect to combine a negative with an adverb such as "barely," "scarcely," or "hardly."

Error: I can't barely stand it.

Correction: I can't stand it.

                   -OR-

                   I can barely stand it.

Skill 12.2   Revise sentences to correct problems relating to sentence construction (e.g., sentence fragments, run-on sentences).

See 9.3

Skill 12.3   Revise sentences to correct problems relating to mechanics (e.g., spelling, punctuation, capitalization).

See 11.1, 11.2, and 11.3

COMPETENCY 13.0   **PRODUCE A WRITTEN SUMMARY OF A GIVEN INFORMATIONAL OR PERSUASIVE PASSAGE.**

- **Organize information into an effective summary of the main ideas of an informational passage, capturing the author's perspective and point of view.**

- **Organize information into an effective summary of the key arguments and supporting details of a persuasive passage, capturing the author's perspective and point of view.**

- **Demonstrate effective paragraph and sentence structure.**

- **Demonstrate command of mechanics, grammar, and usage according to the conventions of Standard English.**

A summary is a streamlined version of the original and is generally five to ten percent of the length of the original, depending on the complexity of the passage and the readers' needs. It should begin by explaining the main purpose and follow with the essential specifics, presented in the same order as the original. It should include conclusions, results, recommendations or implications.

Step 1: Read the passage
At the initial step, you should read the entire passage for the information it presents. Focus on understanding the content. On a second read, you might want to highlight key words or phrases.

Step 2: Determine the main idea
What is the title of the passage? Is there a subtitle? These are usually good indicators of the main idea.

John Updike once wrote an essay titled "Hub Fans Bid Kid Adieu" about Fenway Park and the retirement of Ted Williams. The reader is provided with a clear idea of the topic of the essay.

Another way to determine the main idea is to locate a thesis statement or thesis paragraph.

In paragraph 3, Updike writes:

> *The affair between Boston and Ted Williams has been no mere summer romance; it has been a marriage, composed of spats, mutual disappointments, and, toward the end, a mellowing hoard of shared memories. It falls into three stages, which may be termed Youth, Maturity, and Age; or Thesis, Antithesis, and Synthesis; or Jason, Achilles, and Nestor.*

Look for topic sentences within paragraphs. Following the chronology established in his thesis, Updike begins his following paragraphs thusly:

> **First,** there was the by now legendary epoch when the young bridegroom came out of the West

> **In 1946**, Williams returned from three years as a Marine pilot to the second of his baseball avatars, that of Achilles, the hero of incomparable prowess and beauty who nevertheless was to be found sulking in his tent while the Trojans (mostly Yankees) fought through to the ships.

> After a prime so harassed and hobbled, Williams was granted by the relenting fates a golden twilight.

Step 3: Outline the passage
Get a sense of the scope and organization by identifying the main ideas and supporting points. One way to do this is to note headings and subheadings as well as other graphic elements—such as bullets or sidebars—that highlight information. If no graphic elements are used, make note of paragraph structure and identify sections.

In presenting Updike's complete essay online, Baseball Almanac has written that it "is pleased to present a moving, very detailed, highly informative article about Ted Williams and his life, times, and final moments in Fenway Park." By this introduction, you are given the main idea and scope of this article and can use these as a guide to write your summary.

Also, by using Updike's own thesis statement, you know that the essay proceeds chronologically.

Step 4: Write the summary
Begin your summary by indicating the author's name, the title of the passage and the main idea. Use the present tense and active voice throughout.

.

For example:

> In his essay "Hub Fans Bid Kid Adieu," John Updike pays homage to Fenway Park and baseball great Ted Williams.

Continue the summary in the same order as the original passage. Expand your outline into sentences and provide the reader with a clear and complete summary.

A summary should include the author's main ideas, key arguments, and supporting details. The scope of the summary should match the scope of the original passage.

What should a summary not include?

- **Quotations**. A summary is not a critical analysis that needs to be supported by proof from the original. Further, a summary should not be plagiarized. If you use a quote, then use quotation marks appropriately.
- The **opinions** of the summary writer. A summary is objective. You are presenting the author's perspective; thus you should not intrude upon that with your own comments.
- **New data**. You cannot summarize what hasn't been presented.
- **Irrelevant specifics**. Keep to the main idea and supporting details.
- **Examples, illustrations or examples**. Although these may be useful in understanding the entire piece, they are not necessary in a summary.
- **Background or introductory information** that prepares the reader
- **Footnotes, bibliographies, appendixes, tables or graphs**. These support rather than express conclusions or recommendations.

Step 5: Edit and revise

Review your summary first for content. Does it accurately and completely summarize the original?

Revise for clarity and eliminate wordiness. Avoid the obvious statements, such as "the author believes" or "the author argues."

Review your summary for unity, coherence, and development. Ideas should relate to each other and flow smoothly.

Proof spelling, punctuation, and mechanics.

Your summary should effectively communicate a whole message to the specified audience for the stated purpose.

Does your summary do the following?

- Demonstrate your ability to write on a given topic using language and style appropriate to a given audience, purpose, and occasion.
- Demonstrate your ability to prepare a unified and focused piece of writing.
- Demonstrate your ability to develop and support a topic in a piece of writing.
- Demonstrate your ability to prepare a well-organized piece of writing.
- Demonstrate your ability to use effective sentence structure.
- Demonstrate your ability to apply the standards of edited American English usage.
- Demonstrate your ability to spell, capitalize, and punctuate according to the standards of edited American English.

COMPETENCY 14.0   **PREPARE A DEVELOPED COMPOSITION ON A GIVEN TOPIC USING LANGUAGE CONSISTENT WITH A GIVEN AUDIENCE AND PURPOSE.**

- **Employ effective organizational strategies consistent with the topic and purpose of writing.**

- **Incorporate effective thesis statements, topic sentences, transitions, and conclusions.**

- **Establish and maintain a specific focus through supporting illustrations and examples.**

- **Support an argument with effective logic.**

- **Employ vocabulary consistent with the audience and purpose of the writing sample.**

- **Demonstrate effective paragraph and sentence structure.**

- **Demonstrate command of mechanics, grammar, and usage according to the conventions of Standard English.**

Your composition should effectively communicate a whole message to the specified audience for the stated purpose. You will be assessed on your ability to express, organize, and support opinions and ideas. You will not be assessed on the position you express. You will be asked to:

- Demonstrate the ability to write on a given topic using language and style appropriate to a given audience, purpose, and occasion.
- Demonstrate the ability to prepare a unified and focused piece of writing.
- Demonstrate the ability to develop and support a topic in a piece of writing.
- Demonstrate the ability to prepare a well-organized piece of writing.
- Demonstrate the ability to use effective sentence structure.
- Demonstrate the ability to apply the standards of edited American English usage.
- Demonstrate the ability to spell, capitalize, and punctuate according to the standards of edited American English.

Your composition will be evaluated based on the following criteria:

APPROPRIATENESS: The extent to which the response addresses the topic and uses language and style appropriate to the given audience, purpose, and occasion

MECHANICAL CONVENTIONS: The extent to which words are spelled correctly and to which the response follows the conventions of punctuation and capitalization

USAGE: The extent to which the writing shows care and precision in word choice and is free of usage errors

SENTENCE STRUCTURE: The effectiveness of the sentence structure and the extent to which the sentences are free of structural errors

FOCUS AND UNITY: The clarity with which the response states and maintains focus on the main idea or point of view

ORGANIZATION: The clarity of the writing and the logical sequence of ideas

DEVELOPMENT: The extent to which the response provides statements of appropriate depth, specificity, and/or accuracy

ESSAY GUIDELINES

Even before you select a topic, determine what each prompt is asking you to discuss. This first decision is crucial. If you pick a topic you do not really understand or about which you have little to say, you will have difficulty developing your essay. So take a few moments to analyze each topic carefully *before* you begin to write.

Topic A: A modern invention that can be considered a wonder of the world

In general, the topic prompts have two parts:
* the *SUBJECT* of the topic and
* an *ASSERTION* about the subject.

The **subject** is *a modern invention*. In this prompt, the word *modern* indicates you should discuss something invented recently, at least in this century. The word *invention* indicates you are to write about something created by humans (not natural phenomena such as mountains or volcanoes). You may discuss an invention that has potential for harm, such as chemical warfare or the atomic bomb; or you may discuss an invention that has the potential for good, such as the computer, DNA testing, television, antibiotics, and so on.

The **assertion** (a statement of point of view) is that *the invention has such powerful or amazing qualities that it should be considered a wonder of the world*. The assertion states your point of view about the subject, and it limits the range for discussion. In other words, you would discuss particular qualities or uses of the invention, not just discuss how it was invented or whether it should have been invented at all.

Note also that this particular topic encourages you to use examples to show the reader that a particular invention is a modern wonder. Some topic prompts lend themselves to essays with an argumentative edge, one in which you take a stand on a particular issue and persuasively prove your point. Here, you undoubtedly could offer examples or illustrations of the many "wonders" and uses of the particular invention you chose.

Be aware that misreading or misinterpreting the topic prompt can lead to serious problems. Papers that do not address the topic occur when one reads too quickly or only half understands the topic. This may happen if you misread or misinterpret words. Misreading can also lead to a paper that addresses only part of the topic prompt rather than the entire topic.

To develop a complete essay, spend a few minutes planning. Jot down your ideas, and quickly sketch an outline. Although you may feel under pressure to begin writing, you will write more effectively if you plan your major points.

Prewriting

Before actually writing, you will need to generate content and to develop a writing plan. Three prewriting techniques that can be helpful are:

Brainstorming

When brainstorming, quickly create a list of words and ideas that are connected to the topic. Let your mind roam free to generate as many relevant ideas as possible in a few minutes. For example, on the topic of computers, you may write:

      computer—modern invention
      types—personal computers, microchips in calculators and watches
      wonder—acts like an electronic brain
      uses—science, medicine, offices, homes, schools
      problems—too much reliance; the machines are not perfect

This list could help you focus on the topic and state the points you could develop in the body paragraphs. The brainstorming list keeps you on track and is well worth the few minutes it takes to jot down the ideas. While you have not ordered the ideas, seeing them on paper is an important step.

Questioning

Questioning helps you focus as you mentally ask a series of exploratory questions about the topic. You may use the most basic questions: **who, what, where, when, why, and how.**

"**What** is my subject?"
[computers]

"**What** types of computers are there?"
[personal computers, microchip computers]

"**Why** have computers been a positive invention?"
[act like an electronic brain in machinery and equipment; help solve complex scientific problems]

"**How** have computers been a positive invention?"
[used to make improvements in]
- science (space exploration, moon landings)
- medicine (MRIs, CT scans, surgical tools, research models)
- business (PCs, FAX, telephone equipment)
- education (computer programs for math, languages, science, social studies), and
- personal use (family budgets, tax programs, healthy diet plans)]

"**How** can I show that computers are good?"
[cite numerous examples]

"**What** problems do I see with computers?"
[too much reliance; not yet perfect]

"**What** personal experiences would help me develop examples to respond to this topic?
[my own experiences using computers]

Of course, you may not have time to write out the questions completely. You might just write the words *who, what, where, why,* and *how* and the major points next to each. An abbreviated list might look as follows:

What—computers/modern wonder/making life better
How—through technological improvements: lasers, calculators, CT scans, MRIs.
Where—in science and space exploration, medicine, schools, offices

In a few moments, your questions should help you to focus on the topic and to generate interesting ideas and points to make in the essay. Later in the writing process, you can look back at the list to be sure you have made the key points you intended.

Clustering

Some visual thinkers find clustering to be an effective prewriting method. When clustering, you draw a box in the center of your paper and write your topic within that box. Then, you draw lines from the center box and connect it to small satellite boxes that contain related ideas. Note the cluster below on computers:

SAMPLE CLUSTER

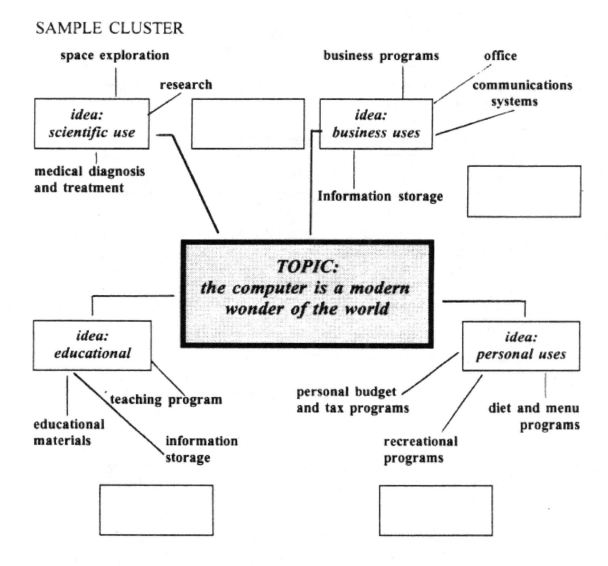

Writing the Thesis

After focusing on the topic and generating your ideas, form your thesis, the controlling idea of your essay. The thesis is your general statement to the reader that expresses your point of view and guides your essay's purpose and scope. The thesis should allow you either to explain your subject or to take an arguable position about it. A strong thesis statement is neither too narrow nor too broad.

Subject and Assertion of the Thesis

From the analysis of the general topic, you saw the topic in terms of its two parts: *subject* and *assertion*. On the exam, your thesis or viewpoint on a particular topic is stated in two important points:

1.   The *SUBJECT* of the paper
2.   The *ASSERTION* about the subject

The **subject of the thesis** relates directly to the topic prompt but expresses the specific area you have chosen to discuss. (Remember, the exam topic will be general and will allow you to choose a particular subject related to the topic.) For example, the computer is one modern invention.

The **assertion of the thesis** is your viewpoint, or opinion, about the subject. The assertion provides the motive or purpose for your essay, and it may be an arguable point or one that explains or illustrates a point of view.

For example, you may present an argument for or against a particular issue. You may contrast two people, objects, or methods to show that one is better than the other is. You may analyze a situation in all aspects and make recommendations for improvement. You may assert that a law or policy should be adopted, changed, or abandoned. As in the computer example, you may also explain to your reader that a situation or condition exists; rather than argue a viewpoint, you would use examples to illustrate your assertion about the essay's subject.

Specifically, the **subject** of Topic A is *the computer*. The **assertion** is that *it is a modern wonder that has improved our lives and that we rely on*. Now you quickly have created a workable thesis in a few moments.

> *The computer is a modern wonder of the world that has improved our lives and that we have come to rely on.*

Guidelines for Writing Thesis Statements

The following guidelines are not a formula for writing thesis statements, but rather are general strategies for making your thesis statement clearer and more effective.

1.   State a *particular point of view* about the topic with both a *subject* and an *assertion.* The thesis should give the essay purpose and scope and thus provide the reader with a guide. If the thesis is vague, your essay may be undeveloped because you do not have an idea to assert or a point to explain. Weak thesis statements are often framed as facts, questions, or announcements:

    a.   Avoid a fact statement as a thesis. While a fact statement may provide a subject, it generally does not include a point of view about the subject that provides the basis for an extended discussion. Example: *Recycling saved our community over $10,000 last year.* This fact statement provides a detail, *not* a point of view. Such a detail might be found within an essay, but it does not state a point of view.

    b.   Avoid framing the thesis as a vague question. In many cases, rhetorical questions do not provide a clear point of view for an extended essay. Example: *How do people recycle?* This question neither asserts a point of view nor helpfully guides the reader to understand the essay's purpose and scope.

    c.   Avoid the "announcer" topic sentence that merely states the topic you will discuss. Example: I *will discuss ways to recycle.* This sentence states the subject, but the scope of the essay is only suggested. Again, this statement does not assert a viewpoint that guides the essay's purpose. It merely "announces" that the writer will write about the topic.

2.   Start with a workable thesis. You might revise your thesis as you begin writing and discover your own point of view.

3.   If feasible and appropriate, perhaps state the thesis in multi-point form, expressing the scope of the essay. By stating the points in parallel form, you clearly lay out the essay's plan for the reader.
Example: *To improve the environment, we can recycle our trash, elect politicians who see the environment as a priority, and support lobbying groups who work for environmental protection.*

4.   Because of the exam time limit, place your thesis in the first paragraph to key the reader to the essay's main idea.

Creating a working outline

A good thesis gives structure to your essay and helps focus your thoughts. When forming your thesis, look at your prewriting strategy—clustering, questioning, or brainstorming. Then, decide quickly which two or three major areas you will discuss. Remember, you must limit *the scope* of the paper because of the time factor.

The **outline** lists those main areas or points as topics for each paragraph. Looking at the prewriting cluster on computers, you might choose several areas in which computers help us, e.g., in science and medicine, business, and education. You might also consider people's reliance on this "wonder" and include at least one paragraph about this reliance. A formal outline for this essay might look like the one below.

I.   Introduction and thesis
II. Computers used in science and medicine
II. Computers used in business
IV. Computers used in education
V.   People's reliance on computers
VI. Conclusion

Under time pressure, however, you may use a shorter organizational plan, such as abbreviated key words in a list. For example:

1. intro: wonders of the computer -OR- a. intro: wonders of computers—science
2. science   b. in the space industry
3. med   c. in medical technology
4. schools   d. conclusion
5. business
6. conclusion

Developing the essay

With a working thesis and outline, you can begin writing the essay. The essay should be in three main sections:

1) The **introduction** sets up the essay and leads to the thesis statement.
2) The **body paragraphs** are developed with concrete information leading from the **topic sentences**.
3) The **conclusion** ties the essay together.

Introduction

Put your thesis statement into a clear, coherent opening paragraph. One effective device is to use a funnel approach, in which you begin with a brief description of the broader issue and then move to a clearly focused, specific thesis statement.

Consider the following introductions to the essay on computers. The length of each is an obvious difference. Read each and consider the other differences.

> Does each introduce the subject generally?
> Does each lead to a stated thesis?
> Does each relate to the topic prompt?

Introduction 1: *Computers are used every day. They have many uses. Some people who use them are workers, teachers, and doctors.*

Analysis: This introduction does give the general topic, computers used every day, but it does not explain what those uses are. This introduction does not offer a point of view in a clearly stated thesis, nor does it convey the idea that computers are a modern wonder.

Introduction 2: *Computers are used just about everywhere these days. I do not think there is an office around that does not use computers, and we use them a lot in all kinds of jobs. Computers are great for making life easier and work better. I do not think we would get along without the computer.*

Analysis: This introduction gives the general topic about computers and mentions one area that uses computers. The thesis states that people could not get along without computers, but it does not state the specific areas the essay discusses. Note, too, the meaning is not helped by vague diction, such as *a lot* or *great.*

Introduction 3: *Each day we either use computers or see them being used around us. We wake to the sound of a digital alarm operated by a microchip. Our cars run by computerized machinery. We use computers to help us learn. We receive phone calls and letters transferred from computers across continents. Our astronauts walked on the moon, and returned safely, all because of computer technology. The computer is a wonderful electronic brain that we have come to rely on, and it has changed our world through advances in science, business, and education.*

Analysis: This introduction is the most thorough and fluent because it provides interest in the general topic and offers specific information about computers as a modern wonder. It also leads to a thesis that directs the reader to the scope of the discussion—advances in science, business, and education.

Supporting Details

If you have a good thesis and a good outline, you should be able to construct a complete essay. Your paragraphs should contain concrete, interesting information and supporting details to support your point of view. As often as possible, create images in your reader's mind. Fact statements also add weight to your opinions, especially when you are trying to convince the reader of your viewpoint. Because every good thesis has an assertion, you should offer specifics, facts, data, anecdotes, expert opinions, and other details to *show* or *prove* that assertion. While *you* know what you mean, your *reader* does not. On the exam, you must explain and develop ideas as fully as possible in the time allowed.

In the following paragraph, the sentences in **bold print** provide a skeleton of a paragraph on the benefits of recycling. The sentences in bold are generalizations that by themselves do not explain the need to recycle. The sentences in *italics* add details to SHOW the general points in bold. Notice how the supporting details help you understand the necessity for recycling.

While one day recycling may become mandatory in all states, right now, it is voluntary in many communities. *Those of us who participate in recycling are amazed by how much material is recycled.* **For many communities, the blue-box recycling program has had an immediate effect.** *By just recycling glass, aluminum cans, and plastic bottles, we have reduced the volume of disposable trash by one-third, thus extending the useful life of local landfills by over a decade. Imagine the difference if those dramatic results were achieved nationwide.* **The amount of reusable items we thoughtlessly dispose of is staggering.** *For example, Americans dispose of enough steel everyday to supply Detroit car manufacturers for three months. Additionally, we dispose of enough aluminum annually to rebuild the nation's air fleet. These statistics, available from the Environmental Protection Agency (EPA), should encourage all of us to watch what we throw away.* **Clearly, recycling in our homes and in our communities directly improves the environment.**

Notice how the author's supporting examples enhance the message of the paragraph and relate to the author's thesis noted above. If you only read the boldface sentences, you have a glimpse at the topic. This paragraph of illustration, however, is developed through numerous details creating specific images: *reduced the volume of disposable trash by one-third, extended the useful life of local landfills by over a decade, enough steel everyday to supply Detroit car manufacturers for three months, enough aluminum to rebuild the nation's air fleet.* If the writer had merely written a few general sentences, as those shown in bold print, you would not fully understand the vast amount of trash involved in recycling or the positive results of current recycling efforts.

End your essay with a brief straightforward **concluding paragraph** that ties together the essay's content and leaves the reader with a sense of its completion. The conclusion should reinforce the main points and offer some insight into the topic, provide a sense of unity for the essay by relating it to the thesis, and signal clear closure of the essay.

Sample Test: Reading Comprehension and Analysis

Read the following passage and answer the questions that follow.

This writer has often been asked to tutor hospitalized children with cystic fibrosis. While undergoing all the precautionary measures to see these children (i.e., scrubbing thoroughly and donning sterilized protective gear for the children's protection), she has often wondered why their parents subject these children to the pressures of schooling and trying to catch up on what they have missed because of hospitalization, which is a normal part of cystic fibrosis patients' lives. These children undergo so many tortuous treatments a day that it seems cruel to expect them to learn as normal children do, especially with their life expectancies being as short as they are.

1. **What is meant by the word "precautionary" in the second sentence?**
    (Average Rigor) (Skill 1.1)

    A. Careful
    B. Protective
    C. Medical
    D. Sterilizing

2. **What is the main idea of this passage?**
    (Average Rigor) (Skill 2.1)

    A. There is a lot of preparation involved in visiting a patient with cystic fibrosis.
    B. Children with cystic fibrosis are incapable of living normal lives.
    C. Certain concessions should be made for children with cystic fibrosis.
    D. Children with cystic fibrosis die young.

3. **What is the author's purpose?**
    (Average Rigor) (Skill 2.4)

    A. To inform
    B. To entertain
    C. To describe
    D. To narrate

4. **What is the author's tone?**
    (Average Rigor) (Skill 4.1)

    A. Sympathetic
    B. Cruel
    C. Disbelieving
    D. Cheerful

5. **Is there evidence of bias in this paragraph?**
    (Rigorous) (Skill 4.1)

    A. Yes
    B. No

6. **Does the author present an argument that is valid or invalid concerning the schooling of children with cystic fibrosis?**
   (Rigorous) (Skill 4.2)

   A. Valid
   B. Invalid

7. **How is the author so familiar with the procedures used when visiting a child with cystic fibrosis?**
   (Easy) (Skill 4.4)

   A. She has read about it.
   B. She works in a hospital.
   C. She is the parent of one.
   D. She often tutors them.

8. **The author states that it is "cruel" to expect children with cystic fibrosis to learn as "normal" children do. Is this a fact or an opinion?**
   (Average Rigor) (Skill 4.4)

   A. Fact
   B. Opinion

Read the following passage and answer the questions that follow.

Disciplinary practices have been found to affect diverse areas of child development such as the acquisition of moral values, obedience to authority, and performance at school. Even though the dictionary has a specific definition of the word "discipline," it is still open to interpretation by people of different cultures.

There are four types of disciplinary styles: assertion of power, withdrawal of love, reasoning, and permissiveness. Assertion of power involves the use of force to discourage unwanted behavior. Withdrawal of love involves making the love of a parent conditional on a child's good behavior. Reasoning involves persuading the child to behave one way rather than another. Permissiveness involves allowing the child to do as he or she pleases and to face the consequences of his/her actions.

9. **What is the meaning of the word "diverse" in the first sentence?**
   (Easy) (Skill 1.1)

   A. Many
   B. Related to children
   C. Disciplinary
   D. Moral

10. **What is the main idea of this passage?**
(Average Rigor) (Skill 2.1)

A. Different people have different ideas of what discipline is.
B. Permissiveness is the most widely used disciplinary style.
C. Most people agree on their definition of discipline.
D. There are four disciplinary styles.

11. **What is the purpose of this selection?**
(Average Rigor) (Skill 2.4)

A. To persuade
B. To describe
C. To inform
D. To tell a story

12. **Name the four types of disciplinary styles.**
(Easy) (Skill 3.3)

A. Reasoning, power assertion, morality, and permissiveness
B. Morality, reasoning, permissiveness, and withdrawal of love
C. Withdrawal of love, permissiveness, assertion of power, and reasoning
D. Permissiveness, morality, reasoning, and power assertion

13. **From reading this passage, we can conclude that**
(Rigorous) (Skill 3.3)

A. The author is a teacher.
B. The author has many children.
C. The author has written a book about discipline.
D. The author has done much research on discipline.

14. **Is this passage biased?**
(Average Rigor) (Skills 4.1)

A. Yes
B. No

15. **The author states "assertion of power involves the use of force to discourage unwanted behavior." Is this a fact or an opinion?**
(Average Rigor) (Skill 4.4)

A. Fact
B. Opinion

Read the following passage and answer the questions that follow.

Rainforests are an endangered habitat on our planet. Found primarily around the Equator, rainforests are categorized as climates with dense humidity, warm temperatures, and high amounts of rainfall—over 80 inches each year.

Extremely important to the Earth's ecology, rainforests provide homes to millions of plants, animals, and food resources. The plants of the rainforest generate rich oxygen for much of the Earth, and if their destruction persists, the damage to the rainforests will cause a dangerous threat to the planet's ecological balance. If the trees and plants fail to grow, the planet is deprived of many of the natural food resources of the rainforest, including cocoa, coffee, sugar cane, and many varieties of nuts, fruits and spices.

Rainforests also recycle air and clean water. The trees capture and remove a large amount of the carbon dioxide in the air. This decreases the temperature of the overall planet, therefore affecting the greenhouse effect, which traps heat in the Earth's atmosphere.

Land seizure is one of the leading threats to the rainforest. If this destruction continues, it will surely result in further critical environmental issues.

16. **Which statement best summarizes this passage?** *(Rigorous) (Skills 5.1, 13.0)*

    A. Rainforests recycle water sources and provide many types of food resources as well.
    B. The Earth consists of many rainforests around its Equator, and they are an important habitat.
    C. Threats to the rainforest, including land seizure, are very dangerous to the rainforests' existence.
    D. Rainforests are currently an endangered habitat and the continued threats to them may be detrimental to the Earth's ecosystems.

17. **Which fact(s) from the passage would most likely not be included in a summary about this topic?** *(Rigorous) (Skill 5.1, 13.0)*

    A. The rainforest traps the heat in the Earth's atmosphere.
    B. The rainforests are an endangered habitat.
    C. There are dangerous threats to the rainforest.
    D. The rainforests play an important role in the balance of the Earth's ecosystems.

Read the following passage and answer the questions that follow.

When Sally Ride became the first American woman to fly in space in 1983, she joined the ranks of other women in her generation who broke traditions and achieved in fields not normally opened for women.

Born in 1951, Ride is part of the Baby Boomer cohort. After World War II ended the birth rate of the United States rose considerably between 1946 and 1964. As the large number of children, called Baby Boomers, reached adolescence and adulthood, they had a great impact on many aspects of American life, including changing the roles of women.

Sally Ride epitomizes this trend in many ways. At a time when many thought that sports were too rough for women, she became a nationally ranked tennis player who considered turning pro. At a time when opportunities for women were limited, Ride was one of many in her generation who not only chose to attend college but also majored in non-traditional fields. She graduated from Stanford University in California in 1973 with degrees in physics and English. This too is remarkable because few women were expected to excel in math and science. She became a rocket scientist in the true sense when she later earned a doctoral degree in astrophysics.

18. **Which pair of synonyms would help students determine the meaning of "cohort"?**
(Easy) (Skill 1.3)

A. epitomizes and trend
B. generation and Baby Boomers
C. traditions and field
D. opportunities and impact

19. **Given the sequence of events in this passage, which detail would be next in order?**
(Average Rigor) (Skill 2.2)

A. Ride made history when she became the first American woman to soar into space.
B. When the National Aeronautics and Space Administration (NASA) placed an ad for scientists and technicians to join the space program, Ride applied.
C. Because the number of women in science remains small, Ride founded Sally Ride Science, a company that promotes interest in science, math, and technology.
D. Before her own mission, she worked as on-orbit capsule communication for two flights.

20. **Which of the following would not support the main idea of the Paragraph 3?**
(Average Rigor) (Skill 2.3)

A. Like other Baby Boomers, Sally Ride was excited about space travel.
B. Because the number of women in science remains small, Ride founded Sally Ride Science, a company that promotes interest in science, math, and technology
C. In 1983, Ride made history when she became the first American woman to soar into space.
D. Of the eight thousand who applied, over one thousand were women. From the total applicants, thirty-five were chosen, and only six were women. Sally Ride was one of the fortunate six.

21. **What type of support do the details in Paragraph 3 provide to the topic sentence "Sally Ride epitomizes this trend in many ways"?**
(Rigorous) (Skill 3.2)

A. Opposition to the argument
B. Implicit cause and effect
C. Explicit cause and effect
D. Inference

22. **The arrangement and relationship of words in sentences or sentence structures best describes**
(Average Rigor) (Skill 4.1)

A. style.
B. discourse.
C. thesis.
D. syntax.

23. **To show the progression of Ride's career, what type of graphic would complement this passage?**
(Rigorous) (Skill 5.3)

A. A bar chart showing the birth rate of children from 1946 to 1964.
B. A time line showing a chronology of events in Ride's life.
C. A map of the orbit of her space flight.
D. A pie chart comparing the number of men and women in the space program.

Multiple Choice

24. **Select the correct order of the following statements to provide the right sequence of events.** *(Easy) (Skill 2.2)*

    1. Josh interviewed with a publishing company.
    2. Josh mailed copies of his resumes to possible employers.
    3. Josh completed a resume course.
    4. Josh began work as a junior copywriter.

    A. 1, 3, 4, 2
    B. 4, 2, 1, 3
    C. 3, 2, 1, 4
    D. 2, 1, 3, 4

25. **The purpose of supporting details in a paragraph is to** *(Easy) (Skill 2.3)*

    A. Summarize the main idea of the passage
    B. Use facts, examples, anecdotes, etc. to show and/or expand on the main idea of the passage
    C. Outline the passage
    D. Provide unnecessary information about the passage

26. **In this paragraph from a student essay, identify the sentence that provides a detail.** *(Rigorous) (Skill 2.2)*

    (1) The poem concerns two different personality types and the human relation between them. (2) Their approach to life is totally different. (3) The neighbor is a very conservative person who follows routines. (4) He follows the traditional wisdom of his father and his father's father. (5) The purpose in fixing the wall and keeping their relationship separate is only because it is all he knows.

    A. Sentence 1
    B. Sentence 3
    C. Sentence 4
    D. Sentence 5

27. **What is the main form of discourse in this passage?** *(Average Rigor) (Skill 2.4)*

    It would have been hard to find a passer-by more wretched in appearance. He was a man of middle height, stout and hardy, in the strength of maturity; he might have been forty-six or seven. A slouched leather cap hid half his face, bronzed by the sun and wind, and dripping with sweat.

    A. Description
    B. Exposition
    C. Narration
    D. Persuasion

28. **Select the statement below that is true about journalistic writing.**
(Average Rigor) (Skill 2.4)

   A. Journalism should contain biased statements.
   B. Journalism should convey information about a person, place, or event in a factual and objective manner.
   C. Using newspapers in the classroom is not a good tool for teaching.
   D. All of the above

29. **Which of the following statements shows a good example of a cause-effect relationship?**
(Average Rigor) (Skill 3.1)

   A. Janice got home late; therefore, she missed her TV program.
   B. Cities have grown very large, so factories have attracted many jobs.
   C. The weather outside was cold, and as a result, Sally opened a window.
   D. Jesse teased the cat because the cat growled.

30. **A composition with no voice will lack the following quality.**
(Rigorous) (Skill 4.1)

   A. Organization
   B. Appeal
   C. Illustrations
   D. Ideas

31. **Bias in testing occurs when**
(Rigorous) (Skill 4.1)

   A. The assessment instrument is not an objective, fair and impartial one for a given cultural, ethnic, or special needs participant.
   B. The testing administrator is biased.
   C. The same test is given with no time considerations or provisions for those in need of more time or those who have handicapping conditions.
   D All of the above

32. **Making inferences from the text means that the reader**
(Rigorous) (Skill 4.2)

   A. is making informed judgments based on available evidence.
   B. is making a guess based on prior experiences.
   C. is making a guess based on what the reader would like to be true of the text.
   D. All of the above.

33. **Which of the following statements describes an analogy?**
(Rigorous) (Skill 4.3)

   A. Analogies compare the likeness of things.
   B. Analogies support that if two things have something in common, they likely have other things in common.
   C. Analogies do not result in false logic.
   D. All of the above

34. **Which of the following is not a fallacy in logic?**
(Rigorous) (Skill 4.3)

A. All students in Ms. Suarez's fourth period class are bilingual.
Beth is in Ms. Suarez's fourth period.
Beth is bilingual.
B. All bilingual students are in Ms. Suarez's class.
Beth is in Ms. Suarez's fourth period.
Beth is bilingual.
C. Beth is bilingual.
Beth is in Ms. Suarez's fourth period.
All students in Ms. Suarez's fourth period are bilingual.
D. If Beth is bilingual, then she speaks Spanish.
Beth speaks French.
Beth is not bilingual.

35. **Mapping the text is an important reading strategy that helps to**
(Rigorous) (Skill 5.1)

A. Connect concepts and ideas in the reading by using colors, lines, pictures, and words to comprehend the meaning of the text
B. Show where the text takes place
C. Connect the reading to other related subjects and texts
D. None of the above

36. **When creating an outline, it is important to teach students**
(Average Rigor) (Skill 5.1)

A. To write neatly
B. To include as much information as possible
C. To include somewhat accurate information
D. How headings and subheadings are used to point out the main ideas in the text

37. **Varying the complexity of a graphic organizer exemplifies differentiating which aspect of a lesson?**
(Rigorous) (Skill 5.1)

A Its content/topic
B. Its environment
C. Its process
D. Its product

38. The following chart shows the yearly average number of international tourists visiting Palm Beach for 1990–1994. How many more tourists that are international visited Palm Beach in 1994 than in 1991?
(Easy) (Skill 5.2)

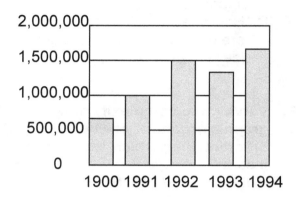

A. 100,000
B. 600,000
C. 1,600,000
D. 8,000,000

39. Which statement is true about George's budget?
(Easy) (Skill 5.2)

A. George spends the greatest portion of his income on food.
B. George spends twice as much on utilities as he does on his mortgage.
C. George spends twice as much on utilities as he does on food.
D. George spends the same amount on food and utilities as he does on mortgage.

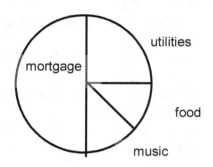

40. For their research paper on the use of technology in the classroom, students have gathered data that shows a sharp increase in the number of online summer classes over the past five years. What would be the best way for them to depict this information visually?
(Rigorous) (Skill 5.3)

A. A line chart
B. A table
C. A pie chart
D. A flow chart

Reading Comprehension and Analysis

Answer Key

1	B	11	C	21	A	31	D
2	C	12	C	22	D	32	A
3	C	13	D	23	B	33	C
4	A	14	B	24	C	34	A
5	A	15	A	25	B	35	A
6	B	16	D	26	C	36	D
7	D	17	A	27	A	37	C
8	B	18	B	28	B	38	B
9	A	19	B	29	A	39	C
10	A	20	A	30	B	40	A

Rigor Table

	Easy 20%	Average 40%	Rigorous 40%
Questions (40)	7, 9, 12, 18, 24, 25, 38, 39,	1, 2, 3. 4, 8, 10, 11, 14, 15, 19, 20, 22, 27, 28, 29, 36	5, 6, 13, 16, 17, 21, 23, 26, 30, 31, 32, 33, 34, 35, 37, 40
TOTALS	8 (20.0%)	16 (40.0%)	16 (40.0%)

Easy: The majority of test takers would get this question correct. It is a simple understanding of the facts and/or the subject matter is part of the basics of an education for teaching English.

Average Rigor: This question represents a test item that most people would pass. It requires a level of analysis or reasoning and/or the subject matter exceeds the basics of an education for teaching English.

Rigor: The majority of test takers would have difficulty answering this question. It involves critical thinking skills such as a very high level of abstract thought, analysis or reasoning, and it would require a very deep and broad education for teaching English.

Rationales for Answers

Reading Comprehension and Analysis

Read the following passage and answer the questions that follow.

This writer has often been asked to tutor hospitalized children with cystic fibrosis. While undergoing all the precautionary measures to see these children (i.e. scrubbing thoroughly and donning sterilized protective gear for the children's protection), she has often wondered why their parents subject these children to the pressures of schooling and trying to catch up on what they have missed because of hospitalization, which is a normal part of cystic fibrosis patients' lives. These children undergo so many tortuous treatments a day that it seems cruel to expect them to learn as normal children do, especially with their life expectancies being as short as they are.

1.   **What is meant by the word "precautionary" in the second sentence?**
     (Average Rigor) (Skill 1.1)

     A. Careful
     B. Protective
     C. Medical
     D. Sterilizing

Answer: B. Protective

The writer uses expressions such as "protective gear" and "children's protection" to emphasize this.

2.   **What is the main idea of this passage?**
     (Average Rigor) (Skill 2.1)

     A. There is a lot of preparation involved in visiting a patient with cystic fibrosis.
     B. Children with cystic fibrosis are incapable of living normal lives.
     C. Certain concessions should be made for children with cystic fibrosis.
     D. Children with cystic fibrosis die young.

Answer: C. Certain concessions should be made for children with cystic fibrosis.

The author states that she wonders, "why parents subject these children to the pressures of schooling" and that "it seems cruel to expect them to learn as normal children do." In making these statements, she appears to be expressing the belief that these children should not have to do what "normal" children do. They have enough to deal with—their illness itself.

3. **What is the author's purpose?**
    (Average Rigor) (Skill 2.4)

    A. To inform
    B. To entertain
    C. To describe
    D. To narrate

Answer: C. To describe

The author is simply describing her experience in working with children with cystic fibrosis.

4. **What is the author's tone?**
    (Average Rigor) (Skill 4.1)

    A. Sympathetic
    B. Cruel
    C. Disbelieving
    D. Cheerful

Answer: A. Sympathetic

The author states, "it seems cruel to expect them to learn as normal children do," thereby indicating that she feels sorry for them.

5. **Is there evidence of bias in this paragraph?**
    (Rigorous) (Skill 4.1)

    A. Yes
    B. No

Answer: A. Yes

The writer clearly feels sorry for these children and gears her writing in that direction.

6. **Does the author present an argument that is valid or invalid concerning the schooling of children with cystic fibrosis?**
    (Rigorous) (Skill 4.2)

    A. Valid
    B. Invalid

Answer: B. Valid

Even though the writer's argument makes good sense to most readers, it shows bias and lacks real evidence.

7. **How is the author so familiar with the procedures used when visiting a child with cystic fibrosis?**
    (Easy) (Skill 4.4)

    A. She has read about it.
    B. She works in a hospital.
    C. She is the parent of one.
    D. She often tutors them.

Answer: D. She often tutors them.

The writer states this fact in the opening sentence.

8. **The author states that it is "cruel" to expect children with cystic fibrosis to learn as "normal" children do. Is this a fact or an opinion?**
    (Average Rigor) (Skill 4.4)

    A. Fact
    B. Opinion

Answer: B. Opinion

The fact that she states that it "seems" cruel indicates there is no evidence to support this belief.

Read the following passage and answer the questions that follow.

Disciplinary practices have been found to affect diverse areas of child development such as the acquisition of moral values, obedience to authority, and performance at school. Even though the dictionary has a specific definition of the word "discipline," it is still open to interpretation by people of different cultures.

There are four types of disciplinary styles: assertion of power, withdrawal of love, reasoning, and permissiveness. Assertion of power involves the use of force to discourage unwanted behavior. Withdrawal of love involves making the love of a parent conditional on a child's good behavior. Reasoning involves persuading the child to behave one way rather than another. Permissiveness involves allowing the child to do as he or she pleases and to face the consequences of his/her actions.

9. **What is the meaning of the word "diverse" in the first sentence?**
    (Easy) (Skill 1.1)

    A. Many
    B. Related to children
    C. Disciplinary
    D. Moral

Answer: A. Many

Any of the other choices would be redundant in this sentence.

10. **What is the main idea of this passage?**
     (Average Rigor) (Skill 2.1)

     A. Different people have different ideas of what discipline is.
     B. Permissiveness is the most widely used disciplinary style.
     C. Most people agree on their definition of discipline.
     D. There are four disciplinary styles.

Answer: A. Different people have different ideas of what discipline is.

The other options cannot be supported.

11. **What is the purpose of this selection?**
    (Average Rigor) (Skill 2.4)

    A. To persuade
    B. To describe
    C. To inform
    D. To tell a story

Answer: C. To inform

Option C is not true; the opposite is stated in the passage. Option B could be true, but we have no evidence of this. Option D is just one of the many facts listed in the passage.

12. **Name the four types of disciplinary styles.**
    (Easy) (Skill 3.3)

    A. Reasoning, power assertion, morality, and permissiveness
    B. Morality, reasoning, permissiveness, and withdrawal of love
    C. Withdrawal of love, permissiveness, assertion of power, and reasoning
    D. Permissiveness, morality, reasoning, and power assertion

Answer: C. Withdrawal of love, permissiveness, assertion of power, and reasoning

This is directly stated in the second paragraph.

13. **From reading this passage, we can conclude that**
    (Rigorous) (Skill 3.3)

    A. The author is a teacher.
    B. The author has many children.
    C. The author has written a book about discipline.
    D. The author has done much research on discipline.

Answer: D. The author has done much research on discipline.

Given all the facts mentioned in the passage, this is the only inference one can make.

14. **Is this passage biased?**
    (Average Rigor) (Skills 4.1)

    A. Yes
    B. No

Answer: B. No

If the reader were so inclined, he could research discipline and find this information.

15. **The author states "assertion of power involves the use of force to discourage unwanted behavior." Is this a fact or an opinion?**
    (Average Rigor) (Skill 4.4)

    A. Fact
    B. Opinion

Answer: A. Fact

The author appears to have done extensive research on this subject.

Read the following passage and answer the questions that follow.

Rainforests are an endangered habitat on our planet. Found primarily around the Equator, rainforests are categorized as climates with dense humidity, warm temperatures, and high amounts of rainfall—over 80 inches each year.

Extremely important to the Earth's ecology, rainforests provide homes to millions of plants, animals, and food resources. The plants of the rainforest generate rich oxygen for much of the Earth, and if their destruction persists, the damage to the rainforests will cause a dangerous threat to the planet's ecological balance. If the trees and plants fail to grow, the planet is deprived of many of the natural food resources of the rainforest, including cocoa, coffee, sugar cane, and many varieties of nuts, fruits and spices.

Rainforests also recycle air and clean water. The trees capture and remove a large amount of the carbon dioxide in the air. This decreases the temperature of the overall planet, therefore affecting the greenhouse effect, which traps heat in the Earth's atmosphere.

Land seizure is one of the leading threats to the rainforest. If this destruction continues, it will surely result in further critical environmental issues.

16. Which statement best summarizes this passage?
(Rigorous) (Skills 5.1, 13.0)

A. Rainforests recycle water sources and provide many types of food resources as well.
B. The Earth consists of many rainforests around its Equator, and they are an important habitat.
C. Threats to the rainforest, including land seizure, are very dangerous to the rainforests' existence.
D. Rainforests are currently an endangered habitat and the continued threats to them may be detrimental to the Earth's ecosystems.

Answer: D. Rainforests are currently an endangered habitat and the continued threats to them may be detrimental to the Earth's ecosystems.

Option A provides more of a detail about the rainforest. Options B and C begin to touch on a summary, but do not quite capture the best summary for the passage. Option D includes that the rainforest is an endangered habitat that is important to the Earth's ecosystem.

17. **Which fact(s) from the passage would most likely not be included in a summary about this topic?**
(Rigorous) (Skill 5.1, 13.0)

 A. The rainforest traps the heat in the Earth's atmosphere.
 B. The rainforests are an endangered habitat.
 C. There are dangerous threats to the rainforest.
 D. The rainforests play an important role in the balance of the Earth's ecosystems.

Answer: A. The rainforest traps the heat in the Earth's atmosphere.

Options B, C, and D all encompass the main idea of the passage—that the rainforests are endangered and the threats to them endanger the balance of ecosystems. Option A is a detail about the rainforest.

Read the following passage and answer the questions that follow.

When Sally Ride became the first American woman to fly in space in 1983, she joined the ranks of other women in her generation who broke traditions and achieved in fields not normally opened for women.

Born in 1951, Ride is part of the Baby Boomer cohort. After World War II ended the birth rate of the United States rose considerably between 1946 and 1964. As the large number of children, called Baby Boomers, reached adolescence and adulthood, they had a great impact on many aspects of American life, including changing the roles of women.

Sally Ride epitomizes this trend in many ways. At a time when many thought that sports were too rough for women, she became a nationally ranked tennis player who considered turning pro. At a time when opportunities for women were limited, Ride was one of many in her generation who not only chose to attend college but also majored in non-traditional fields. She graduated from Stanford University in California in 1973 with degrees in physics and English. This too is remarkable because few women were expected to excel in math and science. She became a rocket scientist in the true sense when she later earned a doctoral degree in astrophysics.

18. **Which pair of synonyms would help students determine the meaning of "cohort"?**
    (Easy) (Skill 1.3)

    A. epitomizes and trend
    B. generation and Baby Boomers
    C. traditions and field
    D. opportunities and impact

Answer: B. Generation and Baby Boomers

In the context of the passage, the term "generation" in the first paragraph introduces the idea of a group. In the second paragraph, the term "Baby Boomer," first used as an adjective and then as a noun, is defined. Using these clues, the reader can determine that "cohort" is a synonym for a group of people.

19. Given the sequence of events in this passage, which detail would be next in order?
(Average Rigor) (Skill 2.2)

   A. Ride made history when she became the first American woman to soar into space.
   B. When the National Aeronautics and Space Administration (NASA) placed an ad for scientists and technicians to join the space program, Ride applied.
   C. Because the number of women in science remains small, Ride founded Sally Ride Science, a company that promotes interest in science, math, and technology.
   D. Before her own mission, she worked as on-orbit capsule communication for two flights.

Answer: B. When the National Aeronautics and Space Administration (NASA) placed an ad for scientists and technicians to join the space program, Ride applied.

This would be the next step in the sequence of becoming an astronaut. Options A and D indicate that Ride was already an astronaut and Option C indicates that she used her flight experience to mentor others.

20. Which of the following would not support the main idea of the Paragraph 3?
(Average Rigor) (Skill 2.3)

   A. Like other Baby Boomers, Sally Ride was excited about space travel.
   B. Because the number of women in science remains small, Ride founded Sally Ride Science, a company that promotes interest in science, math, and technology
   C. In 1983, Ride made history when she became the first American woman to soar into space.
   D. Of the eight thousand who applied, over one thousand were women. From the total applicants, thirty-five were chosen, and only six were women. Sally Ride was one of the fortunate six.

Answer: A. Like other Baby Boomers, Sally Ride was excited about space travel.

The paragraph talks about the ways she defied expectations and did things that women were not expected to do. Option A shows that she was like others whereas the others Options show how she was different.

21. What type of support do the details in Paragraph 3 provide to the topic sentence "Sally Ride epitomizes this trend in many ways"?
(Rigorous) (Skill 3.2)

    A. Opposition to the argument
    B. Implicit cause and effect
    C. Explicit cause and effect
    D. Inference

Answer: A.   Opposition to the argument

The examples refute the idea that women could not participate in sports, would not have as many opportunities, or excel in math or science.

22. The arrangement and relationship of words in sentences or sentence structures best describes
(Average Rigor) (Skill 4.1)

    A. style.
    B. discourse.
    C. thesis.
    D. syntax.

Answer: D.   syntax

Syntax is the grammatical structure of sentences. Style is the manner of expression of writing or speaking. Discourse is an extended expression of thought through either oral or written communication. A thesis is the unifying main idea that can be either explicit or implicit.

23. To show the progression of Ride's career, what type of graphic would complement this passage?
(Rigorous) (Skill 5.3)

    A. A bar chart showing the birth rate of children from 1946 to 1964.
    B. A time line showing a chronology of events in Ride's life.
    C. A map of the orbit of her space flight.
    D. A pie chart comparing the number of men and women in the space program.

Answer: B.   A time line showing a chronology of events in Ride's life

Since this passage relates incidents in her life, a time line showing the chronology of events in Ride's life would provide a useful visual. Option A would help understand the baby boom. Option C would depict just one aspect of her career. Option D does not help illustrate the main idea of this passage.

Multiple Choice

24. **Select the correct order of the following statements to provide the right sequence of events.**
    (Easy) (Skill 2.2)

    1. Josh interviewed with a publishing company.
    2. Josh mailed copies of his resumes to possible employers.
    3. Josh completed a resume course.
    4. Josh began work as a junior copywriter.

    A. 1, 3, 4, 2
    B. 4, 2, 1, 3
    C. 3, 2, 1, 4
    D. 2, 1, 3, 4

Answer: C. 3, 2, 1, 4

This is the only proper sequence of events for these actions.

25. **The purpose of supporting details in a paragraph is to**
    (Easy) (Skill 2.3)

    A. Summarize the main idea of the passage
    B. Use facts, examples, anecdotes, etc. to show and/or expand on the main idea of the passage
    C. Outline the passage
    D. Provide unnecessary information about the passage

Answer: B. Use facts, examples, anecdotes, etc. to show and/or expand on the main idea of the passage

Supporting details are used to expand on the statements in a paragraph. They assist the author in showing support for the main idea of the writing.

26. **In this paragraph from a student essay, identify the sentence that provides a detail.**
    (Rigorous) (Skill 2.2)

(1) The poem concerns two different personality types and the human relation between them. (2) Their approach to life is totally different. (3) The neighbor is a very conservative person who follows routines. (4) He follows the traditional wisdom of his father and his father's father. (5) The purpose in fixing the wall and keeping their relationship separate is only because it is all he knows.

    A. Sentence 1
    B. Sentence 3
    C. Sentence 4
    D. Sentence 5

Answer: C. Sentence 4

Sentence 4 provides a detail to sentence 3 by explaining how the neighbor follows routine. Sentence 1 is the thesis sentence, which is the main idea of the paragraph. Sentence 3 provides an example to develop that thesis. Sentence 4 is a reason that explains why.

27. **What is the main form of discourse in this passage?**
    (Average Rigor) (Skill 2.4)

It would have been hard to find a passer-by more wretched in appearance. He was a man of middle height, stout and hardy, in the strength of maturity; he might have been forty-six or seven. A slouched leather cap hid half his face, bronzed by the sun and wind, and dripping with sweat.

    A. Description
    B. Exposition
    C. Narration
    D. Persuasion

Answer: A. Description

The passage describes the appearance of a person in detail. Narration tells a story. Exposition explains or informs. Persuasion promotes a point of view or course of action.

28. **Select the statement below that is true about journalistic writing.**
    (Average Rigor) (Skill 2.4)

    A. Journalism should contain biased statements.
    B. Journalism should convey information about a person, place, or event in a factual and objective manner.
    C. Using newspapers in the classroom is not a good tool for teaching.
    D. All of the above

Answer: B. Journalism should convey information about a person, place, or event in a factual and objective manner.

Journalistic writing should be free of bias, as it provides information about a person, place, or event using objective facts. Students should be routinely exposed to newspapers in the classroom, as they provide samples of "real-life" print sources.

29. **Which of the following statements shows a good example of a cause-effect relationship?**
    (Average Rigor) (Skill 3.1)

    A. Janice got home late; therefore, she missed her TV program.
    B. Cities have grown very large, so factories have attracted many jobs.
    C. The weather outside was cold, and as a result, Sally opened a window.
    D. Jesse teased the cat because the cat growled.

Answer: A. Janice got home late; therefore, she missed her TV program.

Option A shows the proper cause-effect relationship. Options B, C, and D all have the effect listed first and then the cause, so the relationship is not appropriate.

30. **A composition with no voice will lack the following quality.**
    (Rigorous) (Skill 4.1)

    A. Organization
    B. Appeal
    C. Illustrations
    D. Ideas

Answer: B. Appeal

Voice in writing refers to an author's tone, point of view or manner of communicating. A composition may have good ideas, organization and illustrations or example, but without voice, it will lack character and will not be appealing reading.

31. **Bias in testing occurs when**
    (Rigorous) (Skill 4.1)

    A. The assessment instrument is not an objective, fair and impartial one for a given cultural, ethnic, or special needs participant.
    B. The testing administrator is biased.
    C. The same test is given with no time considerations or provisions for those in need of more time or those who have handicapping conditions.
    D All of the above

Answer: D. All of the above.

Bias in testing occurs when the information within the test or the information required to respond to a multiple choice question or constructed response (essay question on the test) is information that is not available to some test takers who come from a different cultural, ethnic, linguistic or socio-economic background than do the majority of the test takers.

32. **Making inferences from the text means that the reader**
    (Rigorous) (Skill 4.2)

    A. is making informed judgments based on available evidence.
    B. is making a guess based on prior experiences.
    C. is making a guess based on what the reader would like to be true of the text.
    D. All of the above.

Answer: A. Is making informed judgments based on available evidence.

Inferencing is a process that involves the reader making a reasonable judgment based on the information given and engages children to literally construct meaning.

33. **Which of the following statements describes an analogy?**
    (Rigorous) (Skill 4.3)

    A. Analogies compare the likeness of things.
    B. Analogies support that if two things have something in common, they likely have other things in common.
    C. Analogies do not result in false logic.
    D. All of the above

Answer: C. Analogies do not result in false logic.

Analogies can result in false logic and arguments. An example in Skill 4.3 stated

For example, peaches and plums are both fruits that have chemicals good for people to eat. Both peaches and plums are circular in shape; thus, it could be argued by analogy that "because" something is circular in shape, it is fruit and something good for people to eat. However, this analogical deduction is not logical (for example, a baseball is circular in shape but hardly good to eat).

34. **Which of the following is not a fallacy in logic?**
    (Rigorous) (Skill 4.3)

    A. All students in Ms. Suarez's fourth period class are bilingual.
       Beth is in Ms. Suarez's fourth period.
       Beth is bilingual.
    B. All bilingual students are in Ms. Suarez's class.
       Beth is in Ms. Suarez's fourth period.
       Beth is bilingual.
    C. Beth is bilingual.
       Beth is in Ms. Suarez's fourth period.
       All students in Ms. Suarez's fourth period are bilingual.
    D. If Beth is bilingual, then she speaks Spanish.
       Beth speaks French.
       Beth is not bilingual.

Answer: A. All students in Ms. Suarez's fourth period class are bilingual.
Beth is in Ms. Suarez's fourth period.
Beth is bilingual.

The second statement, or premise, is tested against the first premise. Both premises are valid and the conclusion is logical. In B, the conclusion is invalid because the first premise does not exclude other students. In C, the conclusion cannot be logically drawn from the preceding premises – you cannot conclude that all students are bilingual based on one example. In D, the conclusion is invalid because the first premise is faulty.

35. **Mapping the text is an important reading strategy that helps to**
(Rigorous) (Skill 5.1)

   A. Connect concepts and ideas in the reading by using colors, lines, pictures, and words to comprehend the meaning of the text
   B. Show where the text takes place
   C. Connect the reading to other related subjects and texts
   D. None of the above

Answer: A. Connect concepts and ideas in the reading by using colors, lines, pictures, and words to comprehend the meaning of the text

Mapping allows the reader to maneuver through the meaning of a text by connecting concepts and ideas in the reading by using colors, lines, pictures, and words.

36. **When creating an outline, it is important to teach students**
(Average) (Skill 5.1)

   A. To write neatly
   B. To include as much information as possible
   C. To include somewhat accurate information
   D. How headings and subheadings are used to point out the main ideas in the text

Answer: D. How headings and subheadings are used to point out the main ideas in the text

In outlines, concise and accurate headings and subheadings are very important to the outline's effectiveness as a study tool. Students must learn to include the most important information in these headings so they can use it to recall what was most important about what was learned.

37. **Varying the complexity of a graphic organizer exemplifies differentiating which aspect of a lesson?**
    (Rigorous) (Skill 5.1)

    A Its content/topic
    B. Its environment
    C. Its process
    D. Its product

Answer: C. Its process.

Differentiating the process means offering a variety of learning activities or strategies to students as they manipulate the ideas embedded within the lesson concept. For example, students may use graphic organizers, maps, diagrams, or charts to display their comprehension of concepts covered. Varying the complexity of a graphic organizer can very effectively accommodate differing levels of cognitive processing so that students of differing ability are appropriately engaged. Lesson topic and content remain the same, the lesson is still taking place in the same environment and, in most lessons, the graphic organizer is not the product of the lesson

38. **The following chart shows the yearly average number of international tourists visiting Palm Beach for 1990–1994. How many more tourists that are international visited Palm Beach in 1994 than in 1991?**
    (Easy) (Skill 5.2)

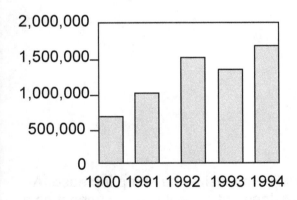

    A. 100,000
    B. 600,000
    C. 1,600,000
    D. 8,000,000

Answer: B. 600,000

The number of tourists in 1991 was 1,000,000 and the number in 1994 was 1,600,000. Subtract to get a difference of 600,000.

39. **Which statement is true about George's budget?**
    (Easy) (Skill 5.2)

    A. George spends the greatest portion of his income on food.
    B. George spends twice as much on utilities as he does on his mortgage.
    C. George spends twice as much on utilities as he does on food.
    D. George spends the same amount on food and utilities as he does on mortgage.

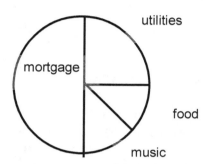

Answer: C. George spends twice as much on utilities as he does on food.

The graph shows that George spends twice as much on utilities as on food.

40. **For their research paper on the use of technology in the classroom, students have gathered data that shows a sharp increase in the number of online summer classes over the past five years. What would be the best way for them to depict this information visually?**
    (Rigorous) (Skill 5.3)

    A. A line chart
    B. A table
    C. A pie chart
    D. A flow chart

Answer: A. A line chart.

A line chart is used to show trends over time and will emphasize the sharp increase. A table is appropriate to show the exact numbers but does not have the same impact as a line chart. Not appropriate are a pie chart which shows the parts of a whole or a flow chart which details processes or procedures.

Sample Test: Writing Knowledge and Proficiency

1. **Which pairing below is the best example of matching an appropriate audience for the type of writing?**
   (Average Rigor) (Skill 6.1)

   A. Creative narrative story to a younger sibling
   B. Friendly letter with slang to a teacher
   C. History essay to a local politician
   D. Business letter to a friend

Choose the most effective word within the context of the sentence.

2. **Many of the clubs in Boca Raton are noted for their _____ elegance.**
   (Average Rigor) (Skill 6.2)

   A. vulgar
   B. tasteful
   C. ordinary

3. **When a student is expelled from school, the parents are usually _____ in advance.**
   (Average Rigor) (Skill 6.2)

   A. rewarded
   B. congratulated
   C. notified

4. **Before appearing in court, the witness was _____ the papers requiring her to show up.**
   (Average Rigor) (Skill 6.2)

   A. condemned
   B. served
   C. criticized

5. **When determining your tone and audience for a piece of writing, which of the following statements is likely to be the least considered?**
   (Rigorous) (Skill 6.2)

   A. What emotional qualities do I want to transmit in this writing?
   B. What choice of language is best suited for my audience?
   C. How lengthy should I make this piece?
   D. What does the person already know about this topic?

Read the following passage and select the best answer.

The local homeless charity is planning to open a new soup kitchen located on Main Street. Their objective is to provide three well-rounded meals to as many as 75 homeless people each day. The kitchen will open at 7:00 in the morning for breakfast and will continue to serve food throughout the day until dinner is over at 6:30 p.m. The organizer of the charity is a woman. Local supermarkets have already agreed to supply food to the charity; however, they are still in need of volunteers to help run the food lines. In addition, further donations of money and food are still needed to supply the patrons adequately.

6. **Which sentence is irrelevant to the information in the passage? (Average Rigor) (Skill 7.2)**

   A. Their objective is to provide three well-rounded meals to as many as 75 homeless people each day.
   B. The organizer of the charity is a woman.
   C. The local homeless charity is planning to open a new soup kitchen located on Main Street.
   D. Local supermarkets have already agreed to supply food to the charity; however, they are still in need of volunteers to help run the food lines.

Select the best answer to the following multiple-choice questions.

7. **The conclusion below is an example of a fallacy. (Rigorous) (Skill 7.4)**

   Premise 1: All horses are mammals.
   Premise 2: All whales are mammals.
   Conclusion: All horses are whales.

   A. True
   B. False

8. **Chose the revision which corrects the sentence problem below.**

   Many factors account for the decline in quality of public education. Overcrowding, budget cutbacks, and societal deterioration, which have greatly affected student learning. (Rigorous) (Skill 8.2)

   A. Overcrowding, budget cutbacks, and societal deterioration, which have greatly affected student learning.
   B. Student learning has been greatly affected by overcrowding, budget cutbacks, and societal deterioration.
   C. Due to overcrowding, budget cutbacks, and societal deterioration, student learning has been greatly affected.
   D. Overcrowding, budget cutbacks, and societal deterioration have affected students learning greatly.

In the sample paragraph below, chose the underlined transition that is not used effectively.

9. Autumn is my favorite time of year. <u>First</u>, the crisp, clean air is refreshing after the humid days of summer. <u>In addition</u>, I love the cinnamon smells in the kitchen of apple pies and cider. I <u>also</u> enjoy the beautiful colors of the trees in autumn, too. <u>In contrast</u>, October brings my favorite holiday, Halloween, when everyone dresses up! <u>In sum</u>, the holidays, smells, and sights make autumn the best time of year.
(Average Rigor) (Skill 8.3)

A. First
B. In addition
C. In contrast
D. In sum

Select the best answer for the following multiple-choice questions.

10. Transitional words and phrases help to
(Average Rigor) (Skill 8.3)

A. Add structure to a text
B. Signal relationships between ideas in a text
C. Enhance the flow of writing
D. All of the above

Choose the underlined word or phrase that is unnecessary within the context of the passage.

11. <u>Considered by many to be</u> one of the worst <u>terrorist</u> incidents <u>on American soil</u> was the bombing of the Oklahoma City Federal Building, which will be remembered <u>for years to come</u>.
(Average Rigor) (Skill 9.2)

A. Considered by many to be
B. terrorist
C. on American soil
D. for years to come

12. The <u>flu</u> epidemic struck <u>most of</u> the <u>respected</u> faculty and students of the Woolbright School, forcing the Boynton Beach school superintendent to close it down <u>for two weeks.</u>
(Rigorous) (Skill 9.2)

A. flu
B. most of
C. respected
D. for two weeks

13. The <u>expanding</u> number of television channels has <u>prompted</u> cable operators to raise their prices, <u>even though</u> many consumers do not want to pay a higher <u>increased</u> amount for their service.
(Easy) (Skill 9.2)

A. expanding
B. prompted
C. even though
D. increased

14. **Climbing to the top of Mount Everest is an <u>adventure. One</u> which <u>everyone—whether</u> physically fit or not—<u>seems</u> eager to try.**
    (Rigorous) (Skill 9.3)

    A. adventure, one
    B. people, whether
    C. seem
    D. No change is necessary

15. **<u>Climbers who</u> take precautions are likely to find the ascent <u>less difficult than</u> the unprepared.**
    (Rigorous) (Skill 10.0)

    A. Climbers, who
    B. least difficult
    C. then
    D. No change is necessary

16. **If climbers are to avoid <u>becoming</u> dehydrated, there <u>is</u> beverages available for <u>them</u> to transport as well.**
    (Easy) (Skill 10.1)

    A. becomming
    B. are
    C. him
    D. No change is necessary

The passage below contains many errors. Read the passage. Then answer each test item by choosing the option that corrects an error in the underlined portion(s). No more than one underlined error will appear in each item. If no error exists, choose "No change is necessary."

Every job <u>places</u> different kinds of demands on <u>their</u> <u>employees</u>. <u>For example,</u> <u>whereas</u> such jobs as accounting and bookkeeping require mathematical <u>ability;</u> graphic design requires creative/artistic ability.

Doing <u>good</u> at one job does not <u>usually</u> guarantee <u>success</u> at another. <u>However</u>, one of the elements crucial to all jobs <u>are</u> especially <u>notable</u>: the chance to accomplish a goal.

The <u>accomplishment</u> of the <u>employees</u> <u>varies</u> according to the job. In many jobs the employees <u>become</u> <u>accustom</u> to the accomplishment <u>provided</u> by the work they do every day.

In medicine, for example, every doctor <u>tests</u> <u>him self</u> by treating badly injured or <u>critically</u> ill people. In the <u>operating room,</u> a team of <u>Surgeons, is</u> responsible for operating on many of <u>these</u> patients. In addition to the feeling of accomplishment that the workers <u>achieve,</u> some jobs also <u>give</u> a sense of identity to the <u>employees'</u>. <u>Profesions</u> like law, <u>education,</u> and sales <u>offer</u> huge financial and emotional rewards. Politicians <u>are</u> public <u>servants: who</u> <u>work</u> for the federal and state governments. President <u>obama</u> is basically employed <u>by</u> the American people to <u>make</u> laws and run the country.

Finally; the contributions that employees make to their companies and to the world cannot be taken for granted. Through their work, employees are performing a service for their employers and are contributing something to the world.

17. However, one of the elements crucial to all jobs are especially notable: the accomplishment of a goal.
(Average Rigor) (Skill 10.1)

A. However
B. is
C. notable;
D. No change is necessary

18. In many jobs the employees become accustom to the accomplishment provided by the work they do every day.
(Average Rigor) (Skill 10.1)

A. became
B. accustomed
C. provides
D. No change is necessary

19. The accomplishment of the employees varies according to the job.
(Rigorous) (Skill 10.1)

A. accomplishment,
B. employee's
C. vary
D. No change is necessary

20. In medicine, for example, every doctor tests him self by treating badly injured and critically ill people.
(Average Rigor) (Skill 10.2)

A. test
B. himself
C. critical
D. No change is necessary

21. Every job places different kinds of demands on their employees.
(Rigorous) (Skill 10.2)

A. place
B. its
C. employes
D. No change is necessary

22. Doing good at one job does not usually guarantee success at another.
(Rigorous) (Skill 10.3)

A. well
B. usualy
C. succeeding
D. No change is necessary

23. Politicians are public servants: who work for the federal and state governments.
(Easy) (Skill 11.1)

A. were
B. servants who
C. worked
D. No change is necessary

24. Finally; the contributions that employees make to their companies and to the world cannot be taken for granted.
(Average Rigor) (Skill 11.1)

   A. Finally,
   B. their
   C. took
   D. No change is necessary

25. for example, whereas such jobs as accounting and bookkeeping require mathematical ability; graphic design requires creative/artistic ability.
(Average Rigor) (Skill 11.1)

   A. For example
   B. whereas,
   C. ability,
   D. No change is necessary

26. In the operating room, a team of Surgeons, is responsible for operating on many of these patients.
(Easy) (Skill 11.2)

   A. operating room:
   B. surgeons is
   C. those
   D. No change is necessary

27. President obama is basically employed by the American people to make laws and run the country.
(Easy) (Skill 11.2)

   A. Obama
   B. to
   C. made
   D. No change is necessary

28. In addition to the feeling of accomplishment that the workers achieve, some jobs also give a sense of self-identity to the employees'.
(Average Rigor) (Skill 11.3)

   A. acheive
   B. gave
   C. employees
   D. No change is necessary

29. Profesions like law, education, and sales offer huge financial and emotional rewards. *(Easy) (Skill 11.3)*

   A. Professions
   B. education;
   C. offered
   D. No change is necessary

30. Mixing the batter for cookies, the cat licked the Crisco from the cookie sheet. **(Rigorous) (Skill 12.1)**

   A. While mixing the batter for cookies
   B. While the batter for cookies was mixing
   C. While I mixed the batter for cookies
   D. While I mixed the cookies

Select the best answer for the following multiple-choice questions.

31. Which of the following should not be included in the opening paragraph of an informative essay? *(Easy) (Skill 14.0)*

   A. Thesis sentence
   B. Details and examples supporting the main idea
   C. A broad general introduction to the topic
   D. A style and tone that grabs the reader's attention

32. Which of the following should not be included in the opening paragraph of a creative writing piece? *(Average Rigor) (Skill 14.0)*

   A. Dialogue
   B. Thesis statement
   C. Introduction of characters and setting
   D. A style and tone that grabs the reader's attention

For the underlined sentence(s), choose the option that expresses the meaning with the most fluency and the clearest logic within the context. If the underlined sentence should not be changed, choose Option A, which shows no change.

33. Selecting members of a President's cabinet can often be an aggravating process. <u>Either there are too many or too few qualified candidates for a certain position, and then they have to be confirmed by the Senate, where there is the possibility of rejection.</u>
(Rigorous) (Skill 14.0)

A. Either there are too many or too few qualified candidate for a certain position, and then they have to be confirmed by the Senate, where there is the possibility of rejection.
B. Qualified candidates for certain positions face the possibility of rejection, when they have to be confirmed by the Senate.
C. The Senate has to confirm qualified candidates who face the possibility of rejection.
D. Because the Senate has to confirm qualified candidates, they face the possibility of rejection.

34. Treating patients for drug and/or alcohol abuse is a sometimes difficult process. <u>Even though there are a number of different methods for helping the patient overcome a dependency, there is no way of knowing which is best in the long run.</u>
(Rigorous) (Skill 14.0)

A. Even though there are a number of different methods for helping the patient overcome a dependency, there is no way of knowing which is best in the long run.
B. Even though different methods can help a patient overcome a dependency, there is no way to know which is best in the long run.
C. Even though there is no way to know which way is best in the long run, patients can overcome their dependencies when they are helped.
D. There is no way to know which method will help the patient overcome a dependency in the long run, even though there are many different ones.

Writing Knowledge and Proficiency

Answer Key

1	A	11	A	21	B	31	B
2	B	12	C	22	A	32	B
3	C	13	D	23	B	33	C
4	B	14	A	24	A	34	B
5	C	15	D	25	C		
6	B	16	B	26	B		
7	A	17	B	27	A		
8	B	18	B	28	C		
9	C	19	C	29	A		
10	D	20	B	30	C		

Rigor Table

	Easy 20%	Average 40%	Rigorous 40%
Questions (40)	13, 16, 25, 27, 32, 33, 35, 37	1, 2, 3, 4, 6, 9, 10, 11, 17, 18, 19, 23, 28, 29, 34, 38,	5, 7, 8, 12, 14, 15, 20, 21, 22, 24, 26, 30, 31,36, 39, 40
TOTALS	8 (20.0%)	16 (40.0%)	16 (40.0%)

Easy: The majority of test takers would get this question correct. It is a simple understanding of the facts and/or the subject matter is part of the basics of an education for teaching English.

Average Rigor: This question represents a test item that most people would pass. It requires a level of analysis or reasoning and/or the subject matter exceeds the basics of an education for teaching English.

Rigor: The majority of test takers would have difficulty answering this question. It involves critical thinking skills such as a very high level of abstract thought, analysis or reasoning, and it would require a very deep and broad education for teaching English.

Rationales for Answers

Writing Knowledge and Proficiency

1. **Which pairing below is the best example of matching an appropriate audience for the type of writing?**
    (Average Rigor) (Skill 6.1)

    A. Creative narrative story to a younger sibling
    B. Friendly letter with slang to a teacher
    C. History essay to a local politician
    D. Business letter to a friend

Answer: A. Creative narrative story to a younger sibling

Of these pairings, A is the best choice, as one might write a creative narrative to entertain a sibling. However, one is unlikely to write an informal friendly letter to a teacher, a history essay to a politician, or a business letter to a friend.

Choose the most effective word within the context of the sentence.

2. **Many of the clubs in Boca Raton are noted for their _____ elegance.**
    (Average Rigor) (Skill 6.2)

    A. vulgar
    B. tasteful
    C. ordinary

Answer: B. tasteful

Tasteful means beautiful or charming, which would correspond to an elegant club. The words *vulgar* and *ordinary* have negative connotations.

3. When a student is expelled from school, the parents are usually _____ in advance.
   (Average Rigor) (Skill 6.2)

   A. rewarded
   B. congratulated
   C. notified

Answer: C. notified

Notified means informed or told, which fits into the logic of the sentence. The words *rewarded* and *congratulated* are positive actions, which do not make sense regarding someone being expelled from school.

4. Before appearing in court, the witness was _____ the papers requiring her to show up.
   (Average Rigor) (Skill 6.2)

   A. condemned
   B. served
   C. criticized

Answer: B. served

Served means given, which makes sense in the context of the sentence. *Condemned* and *criticized* do not make sense within the context of the sentence.

5. When determining your tone and audience for a piece of writing, which of the following statements is likely to be the least considered?
   (Rigorous) (Skill 6.2)

   A. What emotional qualities do I want to transmit in this writing?
   B. What choice of language is best suited for my audience?
   C. How lengthy should I make this piece?
   D. What does the person already know about this topic?

Answer: C. How lengthy should I make this piece?

When determining the tone and audience for writing, answers A, B, and D are all important to consider. The length of the piece (C) is not as important as the other three elements.

Read the following passage and select the best answer.

The local homeless charity is planning to open a new soup kitchen located on Main Street. Their objective is to provide three well-rounded meals to as many as 75 homeless people each day. The kitchen will open at 7:00 in the morning for breakfast and will continue to serve food throughout the day until dinner is over at 6:30 p.m. The organizer of the charity is a woman. Local supermarkets have already agreed to supply food to the charity; however, they are still in need of volunteers to help run the food lines. In addition, further donations of money and food are still needed to supply the patrons adequately.

6. **Which sentence is irrelevant to the information in the passage?**
   (Average Rigor) (Skill 7.2)

   A. Their objective is to provide three well-rounded meals to as many as 75 homeless people each day.
   B. The organizer of the charity is a woman.
   C. The local homeless charity is planning to open a new soup kitchen located on Main Street.
   D. Local supermarkets have already agreed to supply food to the charity; however, they are still in need of volunteers to help run the food lines.

Answer: B. The organizer of the charity is a woman.

Options A, C, and D are all important pieces of information that relate to the opening of the homeless shelter. Option B is an interesting fact to know, but without more detail (such as her name), the fact that the organizer is a woman is irrelevant.

Select the best answer to the following multiple-choice questions.

7. **The conclusion below is an example of a fallacy.**
   (Rigorous) (Skill 7.4)

> <u>Premise 1</u>: All horses are mammals.
> <u>Premise 2</u>: All whales are mammals.
> <u>Conclusion</u>: All horses are whales.

   A. True
   B. False

Answer: A. True

This conclusion is a fallacy, or error in reasoning, as the conclusion is an incorrect one based on insufficient information.

8. **Chose the revision which corrects the sentence problem below.**

   Many factors account for the decline in quality of public education. <u>**Overcrowding, budget cutbacks, and societal deterioration, which have greatly affected student learning**</u>.
   (Rigorous) (Skill 8.2)

   A. Overcrowding, budget cutbacks, and societal deterioration, which have greatly affected student learning.
   B. Student learning has been greatly affected by overcrowding, budget cutbacks, and societal deterioration.
   C. Due to overcrowding, budget cutbacks, and societal deterioration, student learning has been greatly affected.
   D. Overcrowding, budget cutbacks, and societal deterioration have affected students learning greatly.

Answer: B. Student learning has been greatly affected by overcrowding, budget cutbacks, and societal deterioration.

Option B is concise and best explains the causes of the decline in student education. The unnecessary use of *which* in Option A makes the sentence feel incomplete. Option C has weak coordination between the reasons for the decline in public education and the fact that student learning has been affected. Option D incorrectly places the adverb *greatly* after learning, instead of before *affected.*

In the sample paragraph below, chose the underlined transition that is not used effectively.

9. Autumn is my favorite time of year. <u>First</u>, the crisp, clean air is refreshing after the humid days of summer. <u>In addition</u>, I love the cinnamon smells in the kitchen of apple pies and cider. I <u>also</u> enjoy the beautiful colors of the trees in autumn, too. <u>In contrast</u>, October brings my favorite holiday, Halloween, when everyone dresses up! <u>In sum</u>, the holidays, smells, and sights make autumn the best time of year.
(Average Rigor) (Skill 8.3)

   A. First
   B. In addition
   C. In contrast
   D. In sum

Answer: C. In contrast

In this paragraph, the transition *in contrast* is not used properly, as the statement that follows does not contrast with the other supporting sentences. Instead, a transition such as *finally*, would have been more suitable.

Select the best answer for the following multiple-choice questions.

10. Transitional words and phrases help to
    (Average Rigor) (Skill 8.3)

   A. Add structure to a text
   B. Signal relationships between ideas in a text
   C. Enhance the flow of writing
   D. All of the above

Answer: D. All of the above.

Transitions are words or phrases that signal relationships between ideas in a text. Proper use of transitional words and phrases add flow, fluency, and structure to a text.

Choose the underlined word or phrase that is unnecessary within the context of the passage.

11. <u>Considered by many to be</u> one of the worst <u>terrorist</u> incidents <u>on American soil</u> was the bombing of the Oklahoma City Federal Building, which will be remembered <u>for years to come</u>.
     (Average Rigor) (Skill 9.2)

     A. Considered by many to be
     B. terrorist
     C. on American soil
     D. for years to come

Answer: A. Considered by many to be

Considered by many to be is a wordy phrase and unnecessary in the context of the sentence. All other words are necessary within the context of the sentence.

12. The <u>flu</u> epidemic struck <u>most of</u> the <u>respected</u> faculty and students of the Woolbright School, forcing the Boynton Beach school superintendent to close it down <u>for two weeks.</u>
     (Rigorous) (Skill 9.2)

     A. flu
     B. most of
     C. respected
     D. for two weeks

Answer: C. respected

The fact that the faculty might have been *respected* is not necessary to mention in the sentence. The other words and phrases are all necessary to complete the meaning of the sentence.

13. **The expanding number of television channels has prompted cable operators to raise their prices, even though many consumers do not want to pay a higher increased amount for their service.**
(Easy) (Skill 9.2)

    A. expanding
    B. prompted
    C. even though
    D. increased

Answer: D. increased

The word *increased* is redundant with higher and should be removed. All the other words are necessary within the context of the sentence.

14. **Climbing to the top of Mount Everest is an adventure. One which everyone—whether physically fit or not—seems eager to try.**
(Rigorous) (Skill 9.3)

    A. adventure, one
    B. people, whether
    C. seem
    D. No change is necessary

Answer: A. adventure, one

A comma is needed between *adventure* and *one* to avoid creating a fragment of the second part. In Option B, a comma after *everyone* would not be appropriate when the dash is used on the other side of *not*. In Option C, the singular verb *seems* is needed to agree with the singular subject *everyone*.

15. **Climbers who take precautions are likely to find the ascent less difficult than the unprepared.**
    (Rigorous) (Skill 10.0)

    A. Climbers, who
    B. least difficult
    C. then
    D. No change is necessary

Answer: D. No change is necessary

No change is needed. Option A is incorrect because a comma would make the phrase *who take precautions* seem less restrictive or less essential to the sentence. Option B is incorrect because *less* is appropriate when two items—the prepared and the unprepared—are compared. Option C is incorrect because the comparative adverb *than*, not *then*, is needed.

16. **If climbers are to avoid becoming dehydrated, there is beverages available for them to transport as well.**
    (Easy) (Skill 10.1)

    A. becomming
    B. are
    C. him
    D. No change is necessary

Answer: B. are

The plural verb *are* must be used with the plural subject *beverages*. Option A is incorrect because *becoming* has only one m. Option C is incorrect because the plural pronoun *them* is needed to agree with the referent *climbers*.

The passage below contains many errors. Read the passage. Then answer each test item by choosing the option that corrects an error in the underlined portion(s). No more than one underlined error will appear in each item. If no error exists, choose "No change is necessary."

Every job <u>places</u> different kinds of demands on <u>their</u> <u>employees</u>. <u>For example,</u> <u>whereas</u> such jobs as accounting and bookkeeping require mathematical <u>ability;</u> graphic design requires creative/artistic ability.

Doing <u>good</u> at one job does not <u>usually</u> guarantee <u>success</u> at another. <u>However,</u> one of the elements crucial to all jobs <u>are</u> especially <u>notable:</u> the chance to accomplish a goal.

The <u>accomplishment</u> of the <u>employees</u> <u>varies</u> according to the job. In many jobs the employees <u>become</u> <u>accustom</u> to the accomplishment <u>provided</u> by the work they do every day.

In medicine, for example, every doctor <u>tests</u> <u>him self</u> by treating badly injured or <u>critically</u> ill people. In the <u>operating room,</u> a team of <u>Surgeons, is</u> responsible for operating on many of <u>these</u> patients. In addition to the feeling of accomplishment that the workers <u>achieve,</u> some jobs also <u>give</u> a sense of identity to the <u>employees'.</u> <u>Profesions</u> like law, <u>education,</u> and sales <u>offer</u> huge financial and emotional rewards. Politicians <u>are</u> public <u>servants: who</u> <u>work</u> for the federal and state governments. President <u>obama</u> is basically employed by the American people to <u>make</u> laws and run the country.

<u>Finally;</u> the contributions that employees make to <u>their</u> companies and to the world cannot be <u>taken</u> for granted. Through their work, employees are performing a service for their employers and are contributing something to the world.

17. **However, one of the elements crucial to all jobs are especially notable: the accomplishment of a goal.**
    (Average Rigor) (Skill 10.1)

    A. However
    B. is
    C. notable;
    D. No change is necessary

Answer: B. is

The singular verb *is* is needed to agree with the singular subject *one.* Option A is incorrect because a comma is needed to set off the transitional word *however.* Option C is incorrect because a colon, not a semicolon, is needed to set off an item.

18. **In many jobs the employees become accustom to the accomplishment provided by the work they do every day.**
    (Average Rigor) (Skill 10.1)

    A. became
    B. accustomed
    C. provides
    D. No change is necessary

Answer: B. accustomed

The past participle *accustomed* is needed with the verb *become*. Option A is incorrect because the verb tense does not need to change to the past *became*. Option C is incorrect because *provides* is the wrong tense.

19. **The accomplishment of the employees varies according to the job.**
    (Rigorous) (Skill 10.1)

    A. accomplishment,
    B. employee's
    C. vary
    D. No change is necessary

Answer: C. vary

The singular verb *vary* is needed to agree with the singular subject *accomplishment*. Option A is incorrect because a comma after *accomplishment* would suggest that the modifying phrase *of the employees* is additional instead of essential. Option B is incorrect because *employees* is not possessive.

20. **In medicine, for example, every doctor tests him self by treating badly injured and critically ill people.**
    (Average Rigor) (Skill 10.2)

    A. test
    B. himself
    C. critical
    D. No change is necessary

Answer: B. himself

The reflexive pronoun *himself* is needed. (Him self is nonstandard and never correct.) Option A is incorrect because the singular verb *test* is needed to agree with the singular subject *doctor*. Option C is incorrect because the adverb *critically* is needed to modify the verb *ill*.

21. **Every job places different kinds of demands on their employees.**
    (Rigorous) (Skill 10.2)

    A. place
    B. its
    C. employes
    D. No change is necessary

Answer: B. its

The singular possessive pronoun *its* must agree with its antecedent *job*, which is singular also. Option A is incorrect because *place* is a plural form and the subject, *job*, is singular. Option C is incorrect because the correct spelling of employees is given in the sentence.

22. **Doing good at one job does not usually guarantee success at another.**
    (Rigorous) (Skill 10.3)

    A. well
    B. usualy
    C. succeeding
    D. No change is necessary

Answer: A. well

The adverb *well* modifies the word *doing*. Option B is incorrect because *usually* is spelled correctly in the sentence. Option C is incorrect because *succeeding* is in the wrong tense.

23. **Politicians are public servants: who work for the federal and state governments.**
    (Easy) (Skill 11.1)

    A. were
    B. servants who
    C. worked
    D. No change is necessary

Answer: B. servants who

A colon is not needed to set off the introduction of the sentence. In Option A, *were*, is the incorrect tense of the verb. In Option C, *worked*, is in the wrong tense.

24. **Finally; the contributions that employees make to their companies and to the world cannot be taken for granted.**
    (Average Rigor) (Skill 11.1)

    A. Finally,
    B. their
    C. took
    D. No change is necessary

Answer: A. Finally,

A comma is needed to separate *Finally* from the rest of the sentence. *Finally* is a preposition that usually heads a dependent sentence, hence, a comma is needed. Option B is incorrect because *their* is misspelled. Option C is incorrect because *took* is the wrong form of the verb.

25. **for example, whereas such jobs as accounting and bookkeeping require mathematical ability; graphic design requires creative/artistic ability.**
    (Average Rigor) (Skill 11.1)

    A. For example
    B. whereas,
    C. ability,
    D. No change is necessary

Answer: C. ability,

An introductory dependent clause is set off with a comma, not a semicolon. Option A is incorrect because the transitional phrase *for example* should be set off with a comma. Option B is incorrect because the adverb *whereas* functions like *while* and does not take a comma after it.

26. **In the operating room, a team of Surgeons, is responsible for operating on many of these patients.**
    (Easy) (Skill 11.2)

    A. operating room:
    B. surgeons is
    C. those
    D. No change is necessary

Answer: B. surgeons is

Surgeons is not a proper name so it does not need to be capitalized. A comma is not needed to break up *a team of surgeons* from the rest of the sentence. Option A is incorrect because a comma, not a colon, is needed to set off an item. Option C is incorrect because *those* is an incorrect pronoun.

27. **President obama is basically employed by the American people to make laws and run the country.**
    (Easy) (Skill 11.2)

    A. Obama
    B. to
    C. made
    D. No change is necessary

Answer: A. Obama

Obama is a proper name and should be capitalized. Option B, *to*, does not fit with the verb *employed*. Option C uses the wrong form of the verb, *make*.

28. **In addition to the feeling of accomplishment that the workers achieve, some jobs also give a sense of self-identity to the employees'.**
    (Average Rigor) (Skill 11.3)

    A. acheive
    B. gave
    C. employees
    D. No change is necessary

Answer: C. employees

Option C is correct because *employees* is not possessive. Option A is incorrect because *achieve* is spelled correctly in the sentence. Option B is incorrect because *gave* is the wrong tense.

29. **Profesions like law, education, and sales offer huge financial and emotional rewards.**
    (Easy) (Skill 11.3)

    A. Professions
    B. education;
    C. offered
    D. No change is necessary

Answer: A. Professions

Option A is correct because *professions* is misspelled in the sentence. Option B is incorrect because a comma, not a semi-colon, is needed after *education*. In Option C, *offered*, is in the wrong tense.

30. **Mixing the batter for cookies, the cat licked the Crisco from the cookie sheet. (Rigorous) (Skill 12.1)**

    A. While mixing the batter for cookies
    B. While the batter for cookies was mixing
    C. While I mixed the batter for cookies
    D. While I mixed the cookies

Answer: C. While I mixed the batter for cookies.
Options A and E give the impression that the cat was mixing the batter (it is a "dangling modifier"), B that the batter was mixing itself, and D lacks precision: it is the batter that was being mixed, not the cookies themselves.

Select the best answer for the following multiple-choice questions.

31. **Which of the following should not be included in the opening paragraph of an informative essay?**
    (Easy) (Skill 14.0)

    A. Thesis sentence
    B. Details and examples supporting the main idea
    C. A broad general introduction to the topic
    D. A style and tone that grabs the reader's attention

Answer: B. Details and examples supporting the main idea

The introductory paragraph should introduce the topic, capture the reader's interest, state the thesis, and prepare the reader for the main points in the essay. Details and examples, however, should be given in the second part of the essay, so as to help develop the thesis presented at the end of the introductory paragraph, following the inverted triangle method consisting of a broad general statement followed by some information, and then the thesis at the end of the paragraph.

32. **Which of the following should not be included in the opening paragraph of a creative writing piece?**
    (Average Rigor) (Skill 14.0)

    A. Dialogue
    B. Thesis statement
    C. Introduction of characters and setting
    D. A style and tone that grabs the reader's attention

Answer: B. Thesis statement

The introductory paragraph of a creative writing piece would not have a thesis statement, as the thesis is used for expository writing.

For the underlined sentence(s), choose the option that expresses the meaning with the most fluency and the clearest logic within the context. If the underlined sentence should not be changed, choose Option A, which shows no change.

33. **Selecting members of a President's cabinet can often be an aggravating process. Either there are too many or too few qualified candidates for a certain position, and then they have to be confirmed by the Senate, where there is the possibility of rejection.**
    (Rigorous) (Skill 14.0)

    A. Either there are too many or too few qualified candidate for a certain position, and then they have to be confirmed by the Senate, where there is the possibility of rejection.
    B. Qualified candidates for certain positions face the possibility of rejection, when they have to be confirmed by the Senate.
    C. The Senate has to confirm qualified candidates who face the possibility of rejection.
    D. Because the Senate has to confirm qualified candidates, they face the possibility of rejection.

Answer: C. The Senate has to confirm qualified candidates who face the possibility of rejection.

Option C is the most straightforward and concise sentence. Option A is too unwieldy with the wordy *Either...or* phrase at the beginning. Option B does not make clear the fact that candidates face rejection by the Senate. Option D illogically implies that candidates face rejection because they have to be confirmed by the Senate.

34. Treating patients for drug and/or alcohol abuse is a sometimes difficult process. <u>Even though there are a number of different methods for helping the patient overcome a dependency, there is no way of knowing which is best in the long run.</u>
    (Rigorous) (Skill 14.0)

    A. Even though there are a number of different methods for helping the patient overcome a dependency, there is no way of knowing which is best in the long run.
    B. Even though different methods can help a patient overcome a dependency, there is no way to know which is best in the long run.
    C. Even though there is no way to know which way is best in the long run, patients can overcome their dependencies when they are helped.
    D. There is no way to know which method will help the patient overcome a dependency in the long run, even though there are many different ones.

Answer: B. Even though different methods can help a patient overcome a dependency, there is no way to know which is best in the long run.

Option B is concise and logical. Option A tends to ramble with the use of *there are* and the verbs *helping* and *knowing*. Option C is awkwardly worded and repetitive in the first part of the sentence, and vague in the second because it never indicates how the patients can be helped. Option D contains the unnecessary phrase *even though there are many different ones*.

Sample Summary Writing Assignment

Original Article

To rely on distance learning classes for the majority of your coursework is to deny yourself the breadth and depth of a college education. Much is learned inside the classroom that doesn't always relate to the instructor and the course content.

In the physical space, you can more easily share ideas with peers, learn from others' life experiences, and open your mind with the variety of perspectives. Whether taking a math, science, literature or physical education course, you are exposed to a range of people and ideas. Such encounters are rare in online classes.

However, in virtual space, an online class is a solitary venture. You sit alone in front of your computer. You control your time and energy. You roam the course, read, try to understand and follow instructions, and complete activities to further your education. Such solitude is often prized in our people-centered culture. No matter how well designed the course curriculum may be with chat rooms, discussion boards and emails, you are traveling alone, focused on a narrow road, sometimes getting lost and hopefully finding your way again.

You belong to a community of learners. In an online community, you are traveling the road with others but all of you are moving at your own paces, pursuing your own schedules, and arriving and stopping at different places. All are solitary vehicles on different highways heading to the same destination but you each are expending your own time and energy.

In the classroom community, the trip becomes a car pool where you talk, discuss, learn about each other and about the destination to which you are headed. You save time and energy, and arrive better aware of the journey you have taken together.

The success of our society depends on our community. As a learning community, we should temper our desire to finish courses quickly with the desire to learn from courses more completely.

Summary

Online learning is a narrow experience that denies students the opportunities to interact with instructors and each other. Although students may prefer the flexibility and independence of these distance education classes, the learners do not have effective tools to communicate with others. In contrast, students in face-to-face classes can share information and collaborate to achieve success. In pursuing their education, students should consider carefully the disadvantages of online classes.

Evaluation

The 66-word paragraph is an effective summary of the original article of 316 words. It objectively conveys the writer's thesis about the writer's reservation about online learning and summarizes the details (lack of contact, solitary experience, weak communication tools).

Sample Open Response Writing Assignment

Student Learning: Standards-Driven or Project-Based?

In an age of accountability for student learning, many educators assume that sticking to standards and ensuring that each standard is covered explicitly is the safest and most prudent thing to do. However, many educators still believe that engaging students in academic and cross-curricular projects can cover standards, perhaps in a non-linear fashion. Those who believe that project-based instruction is more valuable suggest that students will enjoy their learning more and will still learn many important academic standards in the process. Those who believe that standards-driven learning is more valuable might argue that it is unfair to students not to cover every area on which they will be tested. They might also suggest that teaching standards in a linear fashion will provide greater clarity for students.

In a response written for an audience of teachers, use your knowledge of learners and the learning environment to analyze and discuss the issue of standards-driven and project-based teaching.

RESPONSE

There is no doubt that students must be prepared based on state standards. However, when analyzing state standards, it is important to realize that while standards may look like a bunch of unconnected skills, they really do build upon one another and there is quite a bit of information that overlaps. In my first year as a high school Language Arts teacher, I know that it is important to focus on both standards as well as engaging, meaningful projects. I do not believe that a teacher would have to choose between the two approaches, standards-driven and project-based.

When evaluating what to teach and how to teach it, it is important first to ensure that what is being taught can be defended by the standards. Teachers must make sure that students learn what is required, as students are tested on that material. They are also expected to know that material as they progress to the next grade level.

However, not all students will learn at the same pace and in the same way. Furthermore, if a teacher simply were to "cover" the standards, students would have little context for understanding the material, and it certainly would not be very exciting. Students need to feel that what they are learning is important beyond passing tests. For that reason, developing lessons, units, and projects that take students' varied learning styles into account and draw upon real-world examples and issues will make learning more fun, and it will ensure that all students learn. However, such lessons, units, and projects should also be based on standards so that students have interesting, enjoyable, and student-centered ways of learning the information they are required to know. This method seems to be a more logical approach that combines the positives of both positions.

An example of combining these two approaches, based on a secondary Language Arts classroom, is the teaching of literature. For example, a particular standard might call for students to understand imagery in literature. Another standard might call for students to learn about specific eras in American literature. Another might call for students to learn how to write an analysis of literary techniques. If I were to teach based on standards-driven principles, I would teach all these skills out of context. Yet, if I were to focus simply on a project-based method, I might not hit any of these issues. However, if I were to have students engage in a project that focused on each of these areas and gave them choice in the way they work toward the final project, while giving specialized assistance to those who need it, students will get the opportunity to learn these skills. They will more likely enjoy the process and learn at an appropriate pace.

Combining both approaches seems most logical. While many educators argue that standards-driven instruction is the only way to ensure that students are prepared for testing, doing so alone will provide little opportunity for students to learn in ways that are natural for them. On the other hand, while many educators are convinced that doing anything other than project-based instruction will be boring for students, not paying significant attention to standards will ensure that students are not prepared for the complex academic tasks they will be required to master.

EVALUATION

The assignment asked the candidate to analyze two claims, both at odds with each other. One side, suggesting that standards-driven instruction is more appropriate, seemingly goes against the other side, project-based instruction. Yet the candidate wrote an essay that effectively found the best of both methods. The essay demonstrates a deep knowledge of student learning, as well as contemporary issues of curriculum and instruction. It demonstrated knowledge of student engagement and standards-based instruction. Although the essay did not ask for the candidate to demonstrate the best of both models, its strength lies in the fact that it does indeed show how both methods have some limitations as well as some strengths. Putting both together with a good curricular example was effective.

XAMonline, Inc.
25 First Street, Suite 106
Cambridge, MA 02141
P: 1-800-509-4128
F: 617-583-5552

www.XAMonline.com

2010

VA VCLA, VRA and PRAXIS

PO#:	Store/School:			
Address 1:				
Address 2:				
City, State, Zip:				
Credit Card #:			Exp:	
Phone			Fax:	
Email				

ISBN	TITLE	Qty	Retail	Total
978-1-60787-059-3	Middle School Science 0439		$59.95	
978-1-60787-058-6	ESOL - English to Speakers of Other Languages 0360		$34.95	
978-1-60787-053-1	French Sample Test 0173		$15.00	
978-1-60787-047-0	Physics 0265		$59.95	
978-1-60787-046-3	Earth and Space Sciences 20571		$59.95	
978-1-60787-043-2	Art Sample Test 10133		$19.95	
978-1-60787-041-8	Educational Leadership 0410		$59.95	
978-1-60787-040-1	Physical Education 10091		$59.95	
978-1-60787-039-5	Library Media Specialist 0310		$59.95	
978-1-60787-037-1	Special Education: Teaching Students with Behavioral Disorders/Emotional Disturbance 0371		$21.95	
978-1-60787-035-7	Early Childhood 020, 022		$59.95	
978-1-60787-034-0	Reading 0200, 0201, 0202		$59.95	
978-1-60787-032-6	School Guidance & Counseling 20420		$59.95	
978-1-60787-031-9	Biology 20231, 20232, 20235		$59.95	
978-1-58197-718-9	Spanish 10191, 30194		$59.95	
978-1-58197-691-5	Chemistry 20241 20242, 20245		$59.95	
978-1-58197-269-6	Middle School English Language Arts 10049		$59.95	
978-1-58197-268-9	General Science 10435		$59.95	
978-1-58197-263-4	Middle School Social Studies 0089		$59.95	
978-1-58197-054-8	Government/Political Science 10930		$59.95	
available in April	Middle School Mathematics 0069		*	
available in April	Special Education: Knowledge-Based Core Principles 0351		*	
available in April	Education of Exceptional Students: Core Content Knowledge		*	
available in April	Elementary Education 0011, 0012		*	
available in April	Elementary Educatoin 0014, 0012		*	
available in April	English Language, Literature, and Composition 0041		*	
available in April	Fundamental Subjects 0511		*	
available in April	Mathematics 0061		*	
available in April	ParaPro Assessment 0755		*	
available in April	PPST I: Basic Skills 0710, 0720, 0730		*	
available in April	Principals of Learning and Teaching 0522		*	
available in April	Principals of Learning and Teaching 0524		*	
available in April	Social Studies 0081		*	
978-1-60787-108-8	VCLA Virginia Communication and Literacy Assessment		$59.95	
978-1-60787-109-5	VRA 001 Reading Assessment for Elementary and Special Education Teachers		$59.95	
			SUBTOTAL	
	1 book $8.70, 2 books $11.00. 3+ books $15.00		Ship	
			TOTAL	